Birds of the Lehigh Valley

and Vicinity

2002

Peter G. Saenger
Barbara C. Malt
Kevin F. Crilley

Foreword by Dr. Daniel Klem, Jr.
Muhlenberg College

Maps by Dr. Richard S. Courtney
Kutztown University

Lehigh Valley Audubon Society

Library of Congress Control Number: 2002092673

ISBN: 0-9721409-2-1

Proceeds benefit Lehigh Valley Audubon Society which is a 501C3 nonprofit
organization dedicated to environmental education and conservation.

Published by Lehigh Valley Audubon Society, P. O. Box 290, Emmaus, Pa 18049

Preferred citation:
Saenger, P. G., B. C. Malt, and K. F. Crilley. 2002. Birds of the Lehigh Valley and
Vicinity. Lehigh Valley Audubon Society, Emmaus, Pennsylvania, 152 pp.

Cover:
Chestnut-sided Warbler in a Pin Cherry
by George C. West <www.birchsidestudios.com>

Printed by Rhoads Press, Inc., Allentown, Pa. 18106

To all the Lehigh Valley birders who came and went before us, we owe our deepest gratitude. Their pioneering efforts blazed the trail for all of us who followed.

CONTENTS

FOREWORD

If you live in or near the Lehigh Valley and have an interest in birds, you undoubtedly already know the Lehigh Valley Audubon Society's booklet *Birds of the Lehigh Valley Area*, containing a list of birds, a measure of their relative abundance, and descriptions of select birding sites. This invaluable work was first distributed in 1979 and then updated in 1984 by now local birding legends Bernard L. Morris, Richard E. Wiltraut, and Frederic H. Brock; it has served so many so well for so long. In addition to countless local residents and visitors, for the past 23 years this guide has instructed thousands of my students enrolled in Biology of Birds and Ornithology classes at Moravian and Muhlenberg colleges.

Since 1984, interest in and the documentation of local birds have increased dramatically. To better serve our birds and those who seek to see and study them, it was clear that a current accounting was necessary, and our local Audubon leaders initiated and supported not only an update but an expanded and more sophisticated treatment to build upon their highly successful preceding efforts. The authors of this new book, no longer a booklet, are three extraordinarily knowledgeable Lehigh Valley Audubon Society (LVAS) members and active local birders: Peter G. Saenger, Barbara C. Malt, and Kevin F. Crilley. They enthusiastically volunteered to meet the daunting challenges of preparing this work, and they are to be thanked, praised and congratulated for producing a remarkable publication. Peter Saenger is a gifted instructor and an especially talented birder with extensive local, national, and international experience. Kevin Crilley is an outstanding educator and naturalist within the Montgomery County Park System and possesses exemplary birding knowledge and skills, both locally and nationally. Dr. Barbara Malt is the chair of the Department of Psychology at Lehigh University and has uniquely contributed her many special skills and talents in combination with her commitment, knowledge, and passion for birds.

The heart of this work, like other regional guides, is the species accounts that inform us about what, when, and how many birds occur or are expected in the area. Each species is clearly, concisely, and accurately described in both text and bar graph formats.

To ensure the most accurate accounting for each species, Peter Saenger and Kevin Crilley devoted uncountable hours, many on Sunday afternoons away from their families. The varying quality of records they considered reflected the diversity of interests of those who provided them. Clearly, the joys of birding are different for different people. Documenting an accurate account of the presence and numbers of a species is most rewarding for some. For others it is simply watching the behavior of a common species in the wild or at a feeder. Still others are excited and driven to see a highly sought after species or any rarity to our region. Whatever your pleasure, the joys of birding, like other joys in our lives, are ones that words often fail to adequately convey. By contrast, few other experiences can incite more emotional displeasure and even hostility when a conscientious birder is questioned about an identification he or she reports to another. Innocent as the inquiry may be, for many, a common reaction is a defensive one. Seemingly, a response to a question about one's identification is too often interpreted as a question about one's ability, honesty, even character. In other words, it is difficult for some, seemingly impossible for others, to be objective about such inquiries. Notwithstanding such sensibilities, accuracy is a necessity in a work of this nature to permit the truest accounting of local birdlife. To this end, Saenger and Crilley have done an outstanding job, applying the most rigorous standards based on documented evidence, examining every record in detail and in the case of modern records relying on standards set forth by the Pennsylvania and New Jersey state records committees. In my opinion, they have done so with the utmost respect for these standards and for all those who willingly submitted their reports for public consideration.

Record keeping is a rigorous task if practiced in a way that accurately documents our field observations, interpretations, and ideas. Interest, discipline, and motivation, even a sense of duty, are helpful and some would say necessary traits to properly maintain records of any kind. These universal qualities are particularly essential to advancing our collective knowledge about the birds of our region. It is especially gratifying to see that the authors have devoted a modest but appropriate portion of their work to reminding and instructing us on how important, useful, and rewarding our birding can be for others if we document it completely.

Adding immeasurably to the value of the two previous LVAS offerings, Barbara Malt has more than doubled the number of suggested birding areas to visit in the Lehigh Valley and vicinity, and she has done so effectively, efficiently, and with wonderful style. The detail provided is excellent, and the four-part organization of each description makes finding essential information especially easy. Noteworthy in each site description is comments about what species you can expect to see, and for those birders in search of the unusual, guidance to special species found only in special areas within a site. Also valuable are comments encouraging visitors to further explore a described location, even specific areas within a site, that promise to reward us all by providing new information with expanded coverage. Detailed maps supplement many site descriptions to further aid and ensure that we can readily find and then explore a location in as much detail as we desire.

The LVAS and the authors specifically are to be commended and surely must feel great pride and satisfaction in the *Birds of the Lehigh Valley and Vicinity* for the service and pleasure it will provide anyone interested in the birdlife of this attractive area of eastern North America.

Daniel Klem, Jr., Ph.D., D.Sc.
Professor of Biology, and
Sarkis Acopian Professor of Ornithology and Conservation Biology
Muhlenberg College, Allentown, Pennsylvania

ACKNOWLEDGMENTS

We are grateful to many people whose contributions made this book possible. Our deepest gratitude goes to our families. Kevin's wife Michelle and his daughter Jessica spent many days without him while we worked on the manuscript. Peter's daughter Lauren, who made us lunch and watched Jessica, also forfeited many a day with her father so that we could work on the project. To them, we owe a great many thanks, and we appreciate their patience and understanding. Without their support, we never would have been able to complete this project.

The site guides could not have been written without the efforts of many people who visited sites and submitted draft descriptions. The book benefited greatly from their combined years of experience with the locations described here. We are grateful to the following people for their contributions: John Boyer (Cedar Creek Park and Lake Muhlenberg; Trexler Park), Frederic H. Brock (Leaser Lake; South Mountain Preserve; Martins Creek Environmental Preserve co-author), Dave DeReamus (Little Gap; Smith Gap), Karen Dolan (Sand Island; Martins Creek Environmental Preserve co-author), Amy Francisco (Lake Towhee; Lake Warren; Nockamixon State Park; Quakertown Swamp), Linda Freedman (Monocacy Nature Center), Ted Fritzinger (Whitehall Parkway), Jason Horn (Dorney Landfill), Alan Jennings (Jordan Creek Parkway co-author), Arlene Koch (Oberly Road; Riverview Park), Dan Kunkel (Bake Oven Knob; Bear Rocks), Sheri LaBar (Minsi Lake, Bear Swamp, and East Bangor Dam), Terry Master (Cherry Valley-Portland-Mt. Bethel), Dennis Miller (Graver's Hill), Bernard L. Morris (Little Lehigh Park; Smith Lane; State Gamelands #205), Pauline Morris (Kalmbach Memorial Park), Marty Richter (South Mountain Park), Kathy Sieminski (Albert Road Ponds; Jacobsburg State Park), Brad Silfies (Beltzville State Park; Wild Creek and Penn Forest Reservoirs), Joanne Sora (Jordan Creek Parkway co-author), Kathy Stagl (Pool Wildlife Sanctuary; Reimert Memorial Bird Haven; Rodale Experimental Farm), Leander Stuart (Reservoir Park), Bill Sweeney (Hugh Moore Park), Steve Thorpe (Lehigh Furnace Gap; Lehigh Mountain Uplands), Barry Transue (Mount Bethel Fens), and Billy Weber (Walnutport Area). Thanks are also due to Joanne Sora for help in arranging coverage of the sites and to Barbara Bolle, Linda Freedman, Amy Fransisco, and Joe Zajacek for assistance in confirming and adding additional site details. Dave DeReamus, Steve Thorpe, and LVAS board members provided valuable feedback on the form and content of the site descriptions. Site guides written by the authors: Green Lane Park and Upper Perkiomen Valley Park and Unami Creek Valley (Kevin F. Crilley); Bob Rodale Cycling and Fitness Park, Delaware River, Fogelsville Dam and Quarry, Green Pond, Lehigh River, Merrill Creek Reservoir, Nisky Hill Cemetery, and Wy-Hi-Tuk Park (Barbara C. Malt).

For reviewing and offering substantive suggestions on the annotated species list, we thank the following: Frederic H. Brock, Dave DeReamus, George Franchois, Gary Freed, Bernard L. Morris, and Rick E. Wiltraut.

To Dr. Daniel Klem, Jr., Muhlenberg College, Allentown, PA, we express a special thank you for his guidance and mentorship throughout this project, as well as for allowing us access to his personal reference library.

For production of the maps, we owe special thanks to Dr. Richard S. Courtney of Kutztown University, Kutztown, PA. Map production posed one of the most technically difficult challenges of the book, and without his help, we would surely still be trying to generate the maps. In addition, we owe thanks to Cindy Lippincott from the American Birding Association for her guidance at the beginning of this project with the individual site maps.

For their assistance in gathering U.S. Census Bureau data we thank Jim Adams, Eastern Monroe Public Library, East Stroudsburg, PA.; David Dunlap, Bucks Co. Free Library, Doylestown, PA.; Peg Jordon, Allentown Public Library, Allentown, PA.; and Nathaniel Thomas, Reading Public Library, Reading, PA. For help in gathering reference citations, we thank Eileen C. Mathias, Philadelphia Academy of Natural Sciences library, Philadelphia, PA. and Dr. Keith L. Bildstein, Hawk Mountain Sanctuary Association, Kempton, PA.

We thank all who contributed sighting records, for without records, this book would not have been possible. A complete list of those whose sightings are individually cited is provided below. We also thank all those who have contributed to knowledge of species occurrence in our area but who are not cited in connection with individual records. Their contributions provided much valuable information about species status and distribution.

This project spanned a number of years. If, for whatever reason, we have failed to acknowledge any person who offered assistance in completing this book, we apologize. We are grateful to all who helped.

Peter G. Saenger

Barbara C. Malt

Kevin F. Crilley

Cited Observers

Each of the following individuals is cited within the species text account by his or her initials.

Diane Allison (DA), Peter Bacinski (PB), Frank Bader (FBa), Ian Baldock (IB), Ralph Bardman (RB), Catherine Barlieb (CB), B. Bell (BB), Dick Bell (DBe), Steve Boyce (SBo), John & Nancy Boyer (J&NB), Allen Brady (ABr), David Brandes (DB), Dan Brauning (DBr), Frederic H. Brock (FB), Robert Brody (RBr), Maurice Broun (MB), Jane Bullis (JB), Keith Butler (KB), Gary & Karen Campbell (G&KC), Mark Collie (MC), Albert Conway (AC), Kevin F. Crilley (KFC), David Croll (DC), Walt Culpepper (WC), Dan Dadarrio (DD), Delaware Valley Ornithological Club (DVOC), Dave DeReamus (DDe), Renata Derr (RD), Gerry Dewaghe (GD), Karen Dolan (KD), Dick Dunlap (DDu), Richard Dunlap (RDu), John Ebner (JE), Pauline England (PE), Bill Etter (BE), Cathrine R. Elwell (CRE), Devitch Farbotnik (DF), Steve Farbotnik (SF), John Fedak (JFe), Tom Fegely (TF), Paul Finken (PF), Janet A. Firley (JAF), George Franchois (GAF), Gary Freed (GLF), Linda Freedman (LF), Don Freiday (DFr), Ron French (RFr), Joe Fritz (JF), Ted Fritzinger (TFr), Jack Galm (JG), Dick Gemmell (DG), Dan Gerlach (DGe), Bob Good (BG), Kerry Grim (KG), Al Grout (AG), Ron Grubb (RG), Paul and Anita Guris (P&AGu), Frank Haas (FH), Greg Hanisek (GH), Geoff Hanisek (GeH), Brian Hardiman (BH), David Hawk (DHa), Donald Heintzelman (DH), Scott Heiser (SH), Raymond Hendrick (RH), Durrae Henry (DHe), Armas Hill (AH), Ron Hillegas (RHi), Brian Hillegass (BHi), G. Hitchner (GHi), Bill Hobbs (BHo), Joyce Hoffman (JHof), Ann Hogenboom (AHo), Jeff Hopkins (JHo), Jason Horn (JH), Howard & Eunice Huenecke (H&EH), Alan Jennings (AJ), Mrs. Archibald Johnson (AJo), Richard Kane (RKa), Paul Karner (PK), Rudy Keller (RK), Bernie Kita (BK), Chris Kita (CK), Tim Kita (TK), Daniel Klem, Jr. (DK), Tim Kline (TKl), Katrina Knight (KKn), Arlene Koch (AK), Ken Krannick (KK), Al Kronschnabel (AKr), Leonard Kucinski (LK), Sherri LaBarr (SLa), Jerry Lahr (JL), Ann Lessel (AL), Robert & Anne MacClay (R&AMc), Ralph Mancke (RMan), E. Martin (EMa), Robert Massey (RMas), Earnest Massini (EMas), Terry & Gail Master (T&GM), Terry Master (TM), Lisa Mattioli (LM), Marianna McCabe (MMc), Don McClintock (DMc), Joe McDonald (JMc), Fred Mears (FM), Donald & Elaine Mease (D&EM), Carol Mebus (CMe), Betsy Mescavage (BM), Tracy Meyers (TMe), Adam Miller (AMi), Clint Miller (CM), Debbie Miller (DM), Dennis Miller (DMi), Kathy Miller (KMi), Robert Miller (RM), August & Judy Mirabella (A&JM), August Mirabella (AM), Mark Monroe (MMo), Bernie & Pauline Morris (B&PM), Bernard L. Morris (BLM), John Muddeman (JMu), Bill & Naomi Murphy (B&NM), Mickie Mutchler (MM), Tom Mutchler (TMu), Joe & Esther Pearson (J&EP), John Puschock (JPu), Alton Rauch (AR), Barry Reid (BR), Ken Reiker (KR), Larry Rhoads (LRh), Theodore Rogens (TR), Clement Roth (CR), Sally Roth (SR), Steve Rothenberger (SRo), Hart Rufe (HR), Robert Rufe (RR), Larry Rymon (LR), Patty Sabol (PS), Peter G. Saenger (PGS), Dick Saul (DSa), Michael Schall (MSc), Miriam Schantz (MS), Kathy Sieminski (KS), Brad Silfies (BSi), Joel Silfies (JSi), Jared Silfies (JaSi), Dave Simpson (DS), Jeff Skriletz (JS), Steve Smith (SS), Joanne Sora (JSo), Kathy Stagl (KSt), Phillips B. Street (PBS), Monty Stuart (MSt), R. & L. Thomas (R&LT), Neal Thorpe (NT), Steve Thorpe (ST), Walt Thurber (WT), John Trainer (JT), Barry Transue (BT), Mary Ann Tretter (MAT), *(EW), Ron & Karen Wagner (R&KWa), Billy Weber (BWe),

Babe Webster (BW), Glen A. Weirbach (GW), Dorothy Wiltraut (DW), Rick E. Wiltraut (RW), Frank Windfelder (FW), William Winkelman (WW), Nancy Wisser (NW), Doug Wood (DWo), Gordon Yoder (GY), Richard ZainEldeen (RZ), Joe Zajacek (JZ), and Cathrine Zawaski (CZ).

*One person's initials from the 1984 edition could not be matched to a name. We apologize to (EW), cited in the records for Peregrine Falcon and Tree Swallow, for not being properly identified.

INTRODUCTION

This book is a revision of *Birds of the Lehigh Valley Area* by Morris, Wiltraut, and Brock (1984). Greatly expanded, it reflects the increased knowledge of the avifauna within the region. Our objectives for this revision were twofold: To systematically record the important sighting data for each species and to aid readers in finding birds within the coverage area.

To these ends, the book is divided into three major sections:

1) The Annotated Checklist, with occurrence and abundance status for each species, noteworthy sighting dates, and a brief description of preferred habitat.

2) The Bar Graphs, giving the reader a visual guide to the seasonal occurrence and abundance of each species.

3) The Site Guides, describing fifty of the area's birding locations, including the birds likely to be found at each and detailed driving directions to each location.

Maps are included to help locate each described site, as well as a checklist of all the occurring species, a list of provisional species, and other related information.

The common and scientific names used throughout the book follow the publications of the American Ornithologists' Union (1998, 2000) and their taxonomic treatment of North American birds.

Coverage Area

The area covered by this book is a circle with a 20-mile radius (see map on page 68) centered on the Lehigh Valley International Airport (LVIA). Within this circle are portions of eight counties in Pennsylvania (Lehigh, Northampton, Bucks, Montgomery, Berks, Schuylkill, Monroe, and Carbon) and two counties in New Jersey (Warren and Hunterdon). Four extensions to this circle have been added so that all of Lehigh and Northampton Counties, Green Lane Reservoir and the Unami Creek Valley in Montgomery County, and Penn Forest Reservoir in Carbon and Monroe Counties are included in their entirety. The total area covered is approximately 1,340 square miles.

Physical Features of the Lehigh Valley Area

The geography of the region is varied, supporting a diverse avifauna that includes both northern breeding species such as Magnolia Warblers and southern breeding species such as Carolina Chickadees.

The main geographic features visible from the center of the circle are two ridges, South Mountain to the south and the Kittatinny Ridge to the north. South Mountain extends roughly northeast to southwest through the center of the circle and is characterized by deciduous forest with scattered agricultural areas. Portions of South Mountain exceed 1,000 feet above sea level. The Kittatinny Ridge is the first of a series of ridges to the north. The area from this ridge and northward is mostly wooded with limited farming. It contains most of the area's forested habitat, including large tracts of coniferous forest. The highest elevation, 1,695 feet above sea level, is on the Kittatinny Ridge above Pen Argyl.

Also noteworthy are the Lehigh and Delaware Rivers and their associated watersheds. The Lehigh River flows roughly through the center of the coverage area and joins the Delaware, which cuts through the eastern edge of the circle. Additional aquatic habitats include a number of large man-made reservoirs, smaller lakes and ponds, streams, and very few wetlands. The lowest elevation, about 120 feet, can be found along the Delaware River near Upper Black Eddy. Most of the region drains into the Lehigh and Delaware Rivers.

Agriculture is the predominant rural land use in the limestone valley that extends from Kutztown eastward to the Delaware River and beyond, as well as in the valleys south of South Mountain. Much of this area is characterized by rolling hills and a mixture of farmland and deciduous wood lots.

The area's climate is temperate. The growing season averages 177 days. Winters are comparatively mild; January, the coldest month, averages 27.4 degrees Fahrenheit. The warmest month, July, has an average temperature of 74 degrees Fahrenheit. Rainfall averages 43.7 inches. The average yearly snowfall is 32.1 inches.

Population and Development

The coverage area's population according to the 1980 US Census was 610,771. The 2000 Census puts that figure at 725,232, an increase of over 15% in 20 years.

Development of large areas of former agricultural and forested land has had noticeable impact upon the region's bird life. The Allentown-Bethlehem-Easton metropolitan area is expanding, with large areas of the valley being turned into distribution centers, housing developments, malls, and associated roadways. An example of this sprawl is the loss of the Grim Road area near Trexlertown to development; this site was described in the 1984 edition as a prime location for finding some of the highly sought-after winter field species. Suburban sprawl is reaching the ridges as well, with many of the larger forested areas being fragmented by individual houses and developments.

On the positive side, the area still has much to offer to those interested in the outdoors. Sizeable undeveloped or lightly developed areas remain, some of them permanently protected. The area has a growing number of "green" organizations working collectively toward permanent preservation of additional land.

Annotated Species List

The data contained in the Annotated Species List are the result of sorting through thousands of sighting records, spanning ten counties in Pennsylvania and New Jersey. The data were submitted by more than 200 local observers and published in a number of regional publications.

Records up to and including 1984 are taken directly from *Birds of the Lehigh Valley Area* by Morris, Wiltraut, and Brock (1984). Records from 1985 through 2001 appeared in *The Osprey* (newsletter of the Lehigh Valley Audubon Society), *Pennsylvania Birds, American Birds*, or were from local observers. We rigorously searched out and requested records from every potential source we could identify or those that were brought to our attention by others, and we apologize for any records that were missed.

By publishing all known records in one reference, we hope to encourage others to take notice of their sightings and to understand the importance of collecting data over a long period of time. Equally important is the need for bird watchers to carefully document sightings of rare birds, birds seen outside of their expected season, early and late dates of migrants, and to share this information with others.

To ensure the quality and value of the data contained in this book, we have used the reporting criteria set forth by the Pennsylvania Ornithological Records Committee for all review species (see Appendix A). For all sightings, we have carefully examined and assessed a number of records, and requested additional details from sources where appropriate. In some cases the details of a sighting were incomplete and we used our best judgment. We have done our best to apply all criteria evenly and fairly.

There are 325 species documented for the area. Of these, 258 species are considered to occur regularly, with the remaining 67 classified as Casual or Accidental. The list will surely grow as more and more people pursue the hobby of watching birds and our coverage of the area increases.

Since the 1984 edition, 23 new species have been added to the main list: Pacific Loon, Great Cormorant, Anhinga, Ross's Goose, Barrow's Goldeneye, Mississippi Kite, American Oystercatcher, American Avocet, Whimbrel, Little Gull, Iceland Gull, Lesser Black-backed Gull, Sabine's Gull, Arctic Tern, Rufous Hummingbird, Ash-throated Flycatcher, Violet-green Swallow, Mountain Bluebird, Townsend's Solitaire, Western Tanager, Green-tailed Towhee, Clay-colored Sparrow, and Le Conte's Sparrow.

An additional 26 species are on the Provisional List: Brown Pelican, White Ibis, Pink-footed Goose, Barnacle Goose, Harlequin Duck, Black Rail, Franklin's Gull, Little Gull, Black-headed Gull, Mew Gull, Thayer's Gull, Black-legged Kittiwake, Roseate Tern, Gull-billed Tern, Sooty Tern, Chuck-will's-widow, Black-throated Gray Warbler, Kirtland's Warbler, Bohemian Waxwing, Spotted Towhee, Nelson's Sharp-tailed Sparrow, Harris's Sparrow, Lark Bunting, Black-headed Grosbeak, Boat-tailed Grackle, and Bullock's Oriole. Four of these species were listed as Provisional in the 1984 edition: Brown Pelican, White Ibis, Barnacle Goose, and Lesser Black-backed Gull. Of these, only one has been moved to the main list, the Lesser Black-backed Gull, first reported in 1983, which is now an Uncommon Winter Visitor, with sightings becoming more and more regular.

For each species we include both the common English name and the scientific name. Each species account begins by identifying an Occurrence Status and an Abundance Status (unless the occurrence status is Casual or Accidental, in which case no abundance status is assigned). For species added to the list since the 1984 edition, "New to area" follows the occurrence or abundance status. Important dates based on the occurrence status then follow, and typically a note on the preferred habitat for the species.

The information for each species varies depending on its occurrence status and in general follows these criteria:

- Migrants have an early date for arrival and a late date for departure listed for both the Spring and Fall migration seasons.

- Breeding Birds and Visitors (summer, fall, or winter) have an early arrival and a late departure date, describing when the species is present.

- High counts are included for flocking species or sightings of unusual numbers of a species.

- For Resident and Year-round visitors, high counts are given when applicable.

- Unusual sighting dates for a species are listed, such as a winter sighting for a species usually found only during the breeding season.

- "Unknown" is used where data were unavailable.

When available each sighting record includes the location, exact date, and the observer's initials. The complete list of observers and their respective letter abbreviations can be found in the Observers Cited section in the front of this book.

When many observers were involved in a sighting, the abbreviation "mobs" is used for "many observers".

Definitions

The occurrence status of some species cannot be easily defined by one status category. In these instances, the category that most accurately described the overall occurrence of the species was selected. In some cases, a second modifying status is given to better describe the status.

We use eight abundance categories, which are defined below. As with occurrence status, some species do not fit into one category, and many factors affect abundance at any given moment, such as weather, habitat, and season. The category that best describes abundance under optimal circumstances was assigned.

Together with the seasonal bar graphs, these tools will aid the reader in understanding when a species is most likely to occur and in what relative abundance.

Occurrence Status

One or more of the following eight categories describes the occurrence status of a species. **Resident** is a species that is present year-round and breeds here. Example: Song Sparrow, which is present throughout the year and breeds in the area. Many resident species are most easily observed during the breeding season. **Breeding Bird** is a species that breeds here but is usually not present outside of breeding season. Example: Yellow Warbler, which is present only during breeding season; it breeds here and is absent in winter. **Year-round Visitor** is a species that is known to occur throughout the year but has no confirmed nesting records. Example: Ring-billed Gull. This species may be seen throughout the year but does not nest here. **Visitor** is a species that can be found in the specified season (spring, summer, fall, winter) but does not breed here. These are often post-breeding wanderers, failed breeders, or individuals that for one reason or another visit this area, which is not in their breeding range. Example: Great Egret (a Summer Visitor), is found mainly in late summer, stays for a period of time, and does not breed. **Migrant** is a species that is only seen while passing through the area on migration. Example: Semipalmated Sandpiper, which can be seen in the area in spring and fall while migrating between its breeding grounds to the north and wintering grounds to the south. **Casual** is a species for which there are few records (generally fewer than 10) and its normal range is near enough or its migratory habits are such that it may reoccur. Example: Rufous Hummingbird is a highly mobile western species that occurs with some regularity in the eastern U. S. **Accidental** is a species that has few records (generally 1-3) and a normal range so far away that it is unlikely to reoccur. Example: Anhinga is a species usually found far to the south of our area and there is no expectation this species will reoccur. **Extirpated** is a species that formerly bred here, but no recent records exist. An example is the Northern Bobwhite, which was a resident in years past, but now is believed to occur only as an introduced species.

Abundance Status

One of the following five categories describes the abundance of a species by a careful observer in the <u>appropriate habitat and season</u>. Categories are assigned based upon the peak occurrence of a species. For example, the Sharp-shinned Hawk has an abundance status of Common. This species is common during fall migration but is rare to absent during the summer months. **Common** species are expected to be seen on most field trips. **Fairly Common** species are expected to be seen on more than half of all field trips. **Uncommon** species are expected to be seen on less than half of all field trips. **Rare** species are expected to be seen infrequently, not at all in some years. **Irruptive** species are more common in some years than in others. For example, winter finches can be common one year and absent the following. The word **Local** is used as a modifier of the abundance category for species with extremely limited distribution. For example, there are only a few known sites in our area for finding Red-headed Woodpecker.

Bar Graphs

The bar graphs are a visual representation of the seasonal variation of the occurrence and abundance of each species. They have been drawn to represent the typical status of each species in a given season, in the appropriate habitat and under optimal conditions. They provide more detailed information about the likelihood of seeing a species at any given time than the abundance and occurrence categories and they complement the species text accounts. For example, the Black Duck is a Year-round Visitor that is most observable from October to March. By looking at the bar graph for this species, the reader can determine the likelihood of encountering this species in any given time period.

Different line types are used in the bar graphs to indicate the different abundance categories. The status categories are the same as those used in the species text accounts (Annotated Species List), with the addition of Irregular. The **Irregular** line is used to show historical occurrences of a species where records were insufficient to assign one of the other categories.

Site Guides

The fifty site guides are numbered and cross-referenced to the locator maps on pages 70-73. The guides were prepared to provide four types of information in an easily accessible format. Each guide begins with a **Description** of the area that gives the reader a general overview of the physical environment and habitat type. Next is a section describing the **Birds** expected at the location. If the area is large or contains special sites that warrant added attention, this section is divided into several subsections providing additional details. The third section contains **Directions** to the site, beginning from a major road intersection that can be found on any good regional map. Most of the site guides end with a **Note** section. These notes provide additional information that will aid readers in preparing for a visit to the site (e.g., availability of rest rooms, hours of operation for visitor centers, and safety considerations).

Looking for Birds

New birders should be aware that many of the birds mentioned in the site descriptions cannot be seen at all times of the year. Although some species are year-round residents, some only winter in our area, some only breed here, and some are present only as they pass through in migration. Also, there is no single time period that is "migration" for all species. Some species begin their "fall" migration south as early as July, while others may not move south until November. Even among related species, there can be considerable variation. The peak of fall migration for one species of hawk may be mid-September, but it may be mid-November for another. The site descriptions note when a bird may be present at a location, but birders should carefully consult the **Annotated Species List** and the **Bar Graphs** to determine the best time period for any species of special interest to them.

Many factors can affect how many birds you see on a given day, even at an excellent site. Migration is highly weather-dependent. Any particular day may bring in many birds or few, depending on local, regional and even national weather, and where the birds were previously. Even resident birds may be more visible some days than others. Windy days, for instance, can often make it difficult to see small birds. Time of day also can influence what birds are seen. Songbirds are typically more visible early in the morning; hawks, on the other hand, are seen somewhat later in the morning when they begin to move. Waterfowl may be seen all day, but may roost in one area and feed in another. If you visit a site and find few birds, don't be discouraged; try again another day.

Birding Ethics

The Lehigh Valley Audubon Society endorses the American Birding Association code of ethics and asks all users of this book to abide by its guidelines. The complete ABA code of ethics can be found in Appendix D. In brief, the code requires that birders respect wildlife, its environment, and the rights of others. In any conflict of interest between birds and birders, the welfare of the birds and their environment should come first. For more information on the American Birding Association, visit their web site at <www.americanbirding.org>.

A Few Cautions

Some of the areas described in this book are open to hunting part of the year. We have attempted to note such areas but cannot guarantee that all are mentioned. When visiting sites, heed any signs you may see indicating hunting. During hunting season wear florescent orange and use common sense in these areas. Open season dates vary from year to year. Complete information can be obtained from the Pennsylvania Game Commission web site at <www.pgc.state.pa.us> or by calling 610-926-3136 or (toll free) 1-877-877-9470. For most game species there is no hunting on Sundays, but there are exceptions.

Most lakes, rivers, and creeks are open to fishing at least part of the year. Parking lots and paths along the water can be crowded at peak times, especially the first week of trout season (mid-April). Complete information can be obtained from the Pennsylvania Fish and Boat Commission web site at <www.fish.state.pa.us> or by calling 717-705-7800.

Remember that many people who are not birders enjoy the outdoors as well, and many of them do much to preserve and protect wildlife habitat. Certainly, they should be regarded as allies in conservation and treated with respect.

Many good birding areas have relatively little human traffic, especially early in the morning, and some are fairly remote from major roads or towns. There have been incidents of vandalism in some of the hawk watch site parking lots. Birders should exercise caution when birding in the more isolated areas. A cell phone can be useful in case of an emergency.

Mosquitoes and other biting insects can be a problem in warm weather. We have noted areas where ticks are known to be especially abundant, but they can occur in any natural habitat. Pennsylvania is home to the deer tick, which can carry Lyme disease. Birders should check for ticks and may wish to use insect repellent before going afield.

Keeping Notes

Birding records that document your sightings are not necessary, but they are essential in order for other birders to learn of and to enjoy and evaluate your observations for the benefit of all. We urge all birders to keep a field notebook. Use a notebook that is sturdy such as a medium-sized three-ring binder. Black waterproof ink, now available in ballpoint pens, is best for writing permanent accounts of your observations and other natural history experiences. When preparing each entry, always remember that you are writing not only for yourself, but for others to read. Document each of your field trips with an entry that includes: (1) the site name, (2) directions to the site that include a precise distance from a marked road junction or town, (3) the beginning and ending time you were observing, (4) the distance you traveled on foot or in your vehicle, (5) a description of the habitat that is as detailed as possible, (6) weather conditions that list temperature, wind speed and direction, percent cloud cover, sunny or overcast, general visibility, and the presence or absence of precipitation. Then list the common names and numbers of individuals of each species seen. Just below the species list write a summary line of number of species, number of individuals, and time observing. End your entry by adding your personal comments on the identification of select species seen or your interpretation of any other observations or ideas of interest. For a more detailed set of instructions and additional literature references on why and how to keep a field notebook see Appendices E (Birding Records: How to Keep Them) and C (Rare Bird Report Details).

SPECIES CHECKLIST

Species with (R) following the name are considered rare or accidental in Pennsylvania. It is requested that written details of the sighting, including descriptions, photographs, video or sound recordings, if possible, be sent to the Pennsylvania Ornithological Records Committee (see Appendix C).

___Red-throated Loon
___Pacific Loon (R)
___Common Loon
___Pied-billed Grebe
___Horned Grebe
___Red-necked Grebe
___Eared Grebe
___Double-crested Cormorant
___Great Cormorant (R)
___Anhinga (R)
___American Bittern
___Least Bittern
___Great Blue Heron
___Great Egret
___Snowy Egret
___Little Blue Heron
___Tricolored Heron (R)
___Cattle Egret (R)
___Green Heron
___Black-crowned Night-Heron
___Yellow-crowned Night-Heron
___Glossy Ibis (R)
___Black Vulture
___Turkey Vulture
___Greater White-fronted Goose (R)
___Snow Goose
___Ross's Goose (R)
___Canada Goose
___Brant
___Mute Swan
___Tundra Swan
___Wood Duck
___Gadwall
___Eurasian Wigeon (R)
___American Wigeon
___American Black Duck
___Mallard
___Blue-winged Teal
___Northern Shoveler
___Northern Pintail
___Green-winged Teal
___Canvasback
___Redhead
___Ring-necked Duck
___Greater Scaup
___Lesser Scaup
___Surf Scoter
___White-winged Scoter
___Black Scoter
___Long-tailed Duck (Oldsquaw)
___Bufflehead
___Common Goldeneye

___Barrow's Goldeneye (R)
___Hooded Merganser
___Common Merganser
___Red-breasted Merganser
___Ruddy Duck
___Osprey
___Swallow-tailed Kite (R)
___Mississippi Kite (R)
___Bald Eagle
___Northern Harrier
___Sharp-shinned Hawk
___Cooper's Hawk
___Northern Goshawk
___Red-shouldered Hawk
___Broad-winged Hawk
___Swainson's Hawk (R)
___Red-tailed Hawk
___Rough-legged Hawk
___Golden Eagle
___American Kestrel
___Merlin
___Gyrfalcon (R)
___Peregrine Falcon
___Ring-necked Pheasant
___Ruffed Grouse
___Wild Turkey
___Northern Bobwhite
___Yellow Rail (R)
___King Rail (R)
___Virginia Rail
___Sora
___Purple Gallinule (R)
___Common Moorhen
___American Coot
___Sandhill Crane
___Black-bellied Plover
___American Golden-Plover
___Semipalmated Plover
___Killdeer
___American Oystercatcher (R)
___Black-necked Stilt (R)
___American Avocet
___Greater Yellowlegs
___Lesser Yellowlegs
___Solitary Sandpiper
___Willet
___Spotted Sandpiper
___Upland Sandpiper
___Whimbrel (R)
___Hudsonian Godwit (R)
___Ruddy Turnstone
___Red Knot (R)

___Sanderling
___Semipalmated Sandpiper
___Western Sandpiper
___Least Sandpiper
___White-rumped Sandpiper
___Baird's Sandpiper
___Pectoral Sandpiper
___Dunlin
___Stilt Sandpiper
___Buff-breasted Sandpiper (R)
___Ruff (R)
___Short-billed Dowitcher
___Long-billed Dowitcher
___Common Snipe
___American Woodcock
___Wilson's Phalarope
___Red-necked Phalarope (R)
___Red Phalarope (R)
___Laughing Gull (R)
___Little Gull (R)
___Bonaparte's Gull
___Ring-billed Gull
___Herring Gull
___Iceland Gull
___Lesser Black-backed Gull
___Glaucous Gull
___Great Black-backed Gull
___Sabine's Gull (R)
___Caspian Tern
___Common Tern
___Arctic Tern (R)
___Forster's Tern
___Least Tern (R)
___Black Tern
___Dovekie (R)
___Rock Dove
___Mourning Dove
___Black-billed Cuckoo
___Yellow-billed Cuckoo
___Barn Owl
___Eastern Screech-Owl
___Great Horned Owl
___Snowy Owl
___Barred Owl
___Great Gray Owl (R)
___Long-eared Owl
___Short-eared Owl
___Northern Saw-whet Owl
___Common Nighthawk
___Whip-poor-will
___Chimney Swift
___Ruby-throated Hummingbird

___Rufous Hummingbird (R)
___Belted Kingfisher
___Red-headed Woodpecker
___Red-bellied Woodpecker
___Yellow-bellied Sapsucker
___Downy Woodpecker
___Hairy Woodpecker
___Black-backed Woodpecker (R)
___Northern Flicker
___Pileated Woodpecker
___Olive-sided Flycatcher
___Eastern Wood-Pewee
___Yellow-bellied Flycatcher
___Acadian Flycatcher
___Alder Flycatcher
___Willow Flycatcher
___Least Flycatcher
___Hammond's Flycatcher (R)
___Dusky Flycatcher (R)
___Eastern Phoebe
___Ash-throated Flycatcher (R)
___Great Crested Flycatcher
___Western Kingbird (R)
___Eastern Kingbird
___Scissor-tailed Flycatcher (R)
___Loggerhead Shrike (R)
___Northern Shrike
___White-eyed Vireo
___Yellow-throated Vireo
___Blue-headed Vireo
___Warbling Vireo
___Philadelphia Vireo
___Red-eyed Vireo
___Blue Jay
___American Crow
___Fish Crow
___Common Raven
___Horned Lark
___Purple Martin
___Tree Swallow
___Violet-green Swallow (R)
___Northern Rough-winged Swallow
___Bank Swallow
___Cliff Swallow
___Barn Swallow
___Carolina Chickadee
___Black-capped Chickadee
___Boreal Chickadee (R)
___Tufted Titmouse
___Red-breasted Nuthatch
___White-breasted Nuthatch
___Brown Creeper
___Carolina Wren
___Bewick's Wren (R)
___House Wren
___Winter Wren
___Sedge Wren (R)
___Marsh Wren
___Golden-crowned Kinglet
___Ruby-crowned Kinglet

___Blue-gray Gnatcatcher
___Eastern Bluebird
___Mountain Bluebird (R)
___Townsend's Solitaire (R)
___Veery
___Gray-cheeked Thrush
___Swainson's Thrush
___Hermit Thrush
___Wood Thrush
___American Robin
___Varied Thrush (R)
___Gray Catbird
___Northern Mockingbird
___Brown Thrasher
___European Starling
___American Pipit
___Sprague's Pipit (R)
___Cedar Waxwing
___Blue-winged Warbler
___Golden-winged Warbler
___Tennessee Warbler
___Orange-crowned Warbler
___Nashville Warbler
___Northern Parula
___Yellow Warbler
___Chestnut-sided Warbler
___Magnolia Warbler
___Cape May Warbler
___Black-throated Blue Warbler
___Yellow-rumped Warbler
___Black-throated Green Warbler
___Townsend's Warbler (R)
___Blackburnian Warbler
___Yellow-throated Warbler
___Pine Warbler
___Prairie Warbler
___Palm Warbler
___Bay-breasted Warbler
___Blackpoll Warbler
___Cerulean Warbler
___Black-and-white Warbler
___American Redstart
___Prothonotary Warbler
___Worm-eating Warbler
___Swainson's Warbler (R)
___Ovenbird
___Northern Waterthrush
___Louisiana Waterthrush
___Kentucky Warbler
___Connecticut Warbler
___Mourning Warbler
___Common Yellowthroat
___Hooded Warbler
___Wilson's Warbler
___Canada Warbler
___Yellow-breasted Chat
___Summer Tanager (R)
___Scarlet Tanager
___Western Tanager (R)
___Green-tailed Towhee (R)

___Eastern Towhee
___American Tree Sparrow
___Chipping Sparrow
___Clay-colored Sparrow
___Field Sparrow
___Vesper Sparrow
___Lark Sparrow (R)
___Savannah Sparrow
___Grasshopper Sparrow
___Henslow's Sparrow
___Le Conte's Sparrow (R)
___Seaside Sparrow (R)
___Fox Sparrow
___Song Sparrow
___Lincoln's Sparrow
___Swamp Sparrow
___White-throated Sparrow
___White-crowned Sparrow
___Golden-crowned Sparrow (R)
___Dark-eyed Junco
___Lapland Longspur
___Snow Bunting
___Northern Cardinal
___Rose-breasted Grosbeak
___Blue Grosbeak (R)
___Indigo Bunting
___Painted Bunting (R)
___Dickcissel
___Bobolink
___Red-winged Blackbird
___Eastern Meadowlark
___Yellow-headed Blackbird (R)
___Rusty Blackbird
___Brewer's Blackbird (R)
___Common Grackle
___Brown-headed Cowbird
___Orchard Oriole
___Baltimore Oriole
___Pine Grosbeak (R)
___Purple Finch
___House Finch
___Red Crossbill
___White-winged Crossbill
___Common Redpoll
___Hoary Redpoll (R)
___Pine Siskin
___American Goldfinch
___Evening Grosbeak
___House Sparrow

KEY TO TERMS IN THE ANNOTATED SPECIES LIST

Occurrence Status

One or more of the following eight categories describe the occurrence of a species.

Resident	Present year-round and breeds here.
Breeding Bird	Breeds here, absent during non-breeding season.
Year-round Visitor	Present throughout the year, no confirmed nesting records.
Visitor	Occurs in specified season, does not breed here.
Migrant	Usually only found passing through the area on migration.
Casual	A species with few records (generally fewer than 10) and with a normal range near enough or migratory habits such that it may reoccur.
Accidental	A species with few records (generally 1-3) and a normal range so far away that it is unlikely to reoccur.
Extirpated	A species that formerly bred here, but no recent records exist.

Abundance

The following five categories describe the abundance of a species for a careful observer in the <u>appropriate habitat and season</u>.

Common	Expected to be seen on most field trips.
Fairly Common	Expected to be seen on more than half of all field trips.
Uncommon	Expected to be seen on less than half of all field trips.
Rare	Expected to be seen infrequently, some years not at all.
Irruptive	More common in some years than in others.

The word **Local** is used as a modifier of the abundance category for species with extremely limited distribution. For example, there are only a few known sites in our area for finding the Red-headed Woodpecker. If "**under review**" follows the initials of an observer, the sighting has been submitted to the Pennsylvania Records Committee and pending review.

For a complete explanation of the information contained within each species text account, see Introduction, Annotated Species List (page 14).

Red-throated Loon   *Gavia stellata*
MIGRANT. RARE. Spring: Green Lane Reservoir 3/20/83 (BSi, SBo) - Leaser Lake 6/15/80 (KK). Fall: Nockamixon State Park 11/8/00 (DF) – Beltzville State Park 12/31/91 (RW). High count: 7-Nockamixon State Park 4/23/00 (DF). One winter record: Beltzville State Park 1/26/99 (RW). Usually found on larger lakes and rivers.

Pacific Loon   *Gavia pacifica*
CASUAL. New to area. At least four area records: First recorded Merrill Creek Reservoir 11/15-19/88 (GH, mobs). Additional records: Merrill Creek Reservoir 5/11/92 (PB, DFr in Boyle et al. 1992), Green Lane Reservoir 4/29/96 (JH-photo, mobs), and Nockamixon State Park 4/23/00 (DF, JH). Usually found on larger lakes and rivers.

Common Loon   *Gavia immer*
MIGRANT. UNCOMMON. Spring: Nockamixon State Park 3/23/97 (SF) - Nockamixon State Park 6/4/91 (SF). Fall: Beltzville State Park 9/19/89 (RW) - Beltzville State Park 1/20-2/4/99 (RW). High count: 471-Penn Forest Reservoir 4/21/92 (BSi). A few individuals may linger well into winter. One known February record: Martins Creek 2/25/00 (RW). At least 12 summer records, including: Penn Forest Reservoir 1979-1986 (LR, BLM), with breeding in 1982 (LR). Usually found on larger lakes and rivers.

Pied-billed Grebe   *Podilymbus podiceps*
MIGRANT, WINTER VISITOR. UNCOMMON. At least 6 summer records, including two birds courting East Bangor Dam 5/28/78 (RW) and a bird with young on its back Minsi Lake 7/82 (BSi). High count: 27-Minsi Lake 4/15/78 (RW). A few winter records. Possible on any body of water.

Horned Grebe   *Podiceps auritus*
MIGRANT. UNCOMMON. Spring: Green Lane Reservoir 2/18/98 (KFC) - Nockamixon State Park 5/20/91 (SF). Fall: Green Lane Reservoir 10/3/93 (J&NB) - 20-Beltzville State Park 12/30/83 (SBo, RW). High count: 38-Nockamixon State Park 4/6/90 (SF). At least seven winter records. Usually found on larger lakes and rivers.

Red-necked Grebe   *Podiceps grisegena*
MIGRANT. RARE. Spring: Delaware River 2/14/77 (RW) - East Bangor Dam 5/12/89 (SBo). Fall: Green Lane Reservoir 10/29/83 (GLF) - Nockamixon State Park 12/5-25/91 (SF, B&NM). High count: 13-Green Lane Reservoir 3/28/59 (PBS). One winter record: Wild Creek Reservoir 1/1/86 (SBo, RW, GY). Usually found on larger lakes and rivers.

Eared Grebe   *Podiceps nigricollis*
ACCIDENTAL. Two records: Green Lane Reservoir 4/8/62 (J&EP) and Green Lane Reservoir 10/16/97 (JH, mobs).

Double-crested Cormorant   *Phalacrocorax auritus*
MIGRANT, SUMMER VISITOR. FAIRLY COMMON. Sightings increasing. Early date: Green Lane Reservoir 3/24/01 (GAF). Late date: Green Lane Reservoir 12/16/01 (GLF). High count: 375-Little Gap Bird Observatory 10/16/95. Three winter records: Revere 1/16/1990 (SF), Martins Creek 12/31/91 (DDe, AK, RW), and Easton 1/2/2000 (DB, DDe). Usually found on larger lakes and rivers.

Great Cormorant   *Phalacrocorax carbo*
WINTER VISITOR. RARE. New to area. At least 11 records. First recorded: Morgan's Hill 4/26/88 (DDe). Early date: Green Lane Reservoir 10/22/97 (GAF). Late date: Martins Creek 5/30/00 (RW). High count: 4-Martins Creek 4/15/99 (RW, mobs).

Anhinga *Anhinga anhinga*
ACCIDENTAL. New to area. One record: Unami Creek Valley 5/15/96 (AM). Freed, G. L. 1996.
Local notes: Montgomery County, Pennsylvania Birds 10:103.

American Bittern *Botaurus lentiginosus*
MIGRANT. RARE and declining. Spring: Green Lane Reservoir 3/26/97 (KFC) – 7 (high count)-
Quakertown Swamp 5/1/00 (DF, SF, IB). Fall: Green Lane Reservoir 10/16/01 (KFC) - Green Lane
Reservoir 12/7/95 (KFC). Found in densely vegetated wetlands.

Least Bittern *Ixobrychus exilis*
MIGRANT. RARE. Spring: Green Lane Reservoir 4/16/97 (JH-photo) - Unknown. Fall: Unknown -
11/22/54 (CB). One breeding record: Lake Warren 1985 (SF). Found in densely vegetated wetlands.

Great Blue Heron *Ardea herodias*
RESIDENT. FAIRLY COMMON. First nested in area at Quakertown Swamp 1994 (A&JM). 50 nesting
pair at Quakertown Swamp in 1999 (A&JM). Also nesting colonies at Nockamixon State Park
(since 2000), along the Lehigh River between Allentown and Fountain Hill, and two nests reported
at the Fogelsville Quarry. Most often found near water and in meadows.

Great Egret *Ardea albus*
SUMMER VISITOR. UNCOMMON. Most often seen in August and September. Early date: Green Lane
Reservoir 3/29/96 (KFC). Late date: Martins Creek 11/18/99 (RW). High count: 24-Green Lane
Reservoir 8/4/85 (GLF). Four winter records. Found along lakes and stream banks.

Snowy Egret *Egretta thula*
SUMMER VISITOR. RARE and declining. Most often seen in August and September. Early date: Albert
Road Ponds 3/29/93 (KS). Late date: 10/10/82 (BLM). High count: 13-Green Lane Reservoir
8/14/83 (GLF, BLM). Found along lakes and stream banks.

Little Blue Heron *Egretta caerulea*
SUMMER VISITOR. RARE. Early date: Spring Creek 4/8/84 (SS). Late date: Upper Perkiomen Valley
Park 10/28/01 (P & AG). High count: 6-Green Lane Reservoir 7/27/86 (GLF, GAF). Found along
lakes and stream banks.

Tricolored Heron *Egretta tricolor*
ACCIDENTAL. Three records (all from Green Lane Reservoir): 8/20-27/76 (RBr, GAF), 7/19-21/85
(GAF, GLF), 7/23-9/10/88 (KFC, mobs).

Cattle Egret *Bubulcus ibis*
SUMMER VISITOR. RARE and declining. First documented: Spring Creek 5/4/60 (CM). Early date:
4/5/80 (JMc). Late date: 12/12/66 (MS). High count: 14-Catasauqua 5/13/80 (T&GM). Found in
pastures, fields, and along lake shores.

Green Heron *Butorides virescens*
BREEDING BIRD. FAIRLY COMMON. Early date: 3/11/67 (JS). Late date: Green Lane Reservoir
10/24/96 (KFC). Three winter records: 12/7/64 (DH), Bethlehem-Hellertown-Easton Christmas
Bird Count (1973, 1974). Prefers smaller bodies of water, also found along edges of lakes, streams,
and rivers.

Black-crowned Night-Heron *Nycticorax nycticorax*
VISITOR. RARE. Formerly more common. Early date: Milford Twp. 3/10/90 (RH). Late date:
Martins Creek 10/14/90 (AK). High count: *77-Milford Twp. 7/22/78 (A&JM). One December
record: Salisbury Twp. 12/29/79 (FB). Two February records: 2/1/78 Dorney Pond (BLM), 2/7/79
Bethlehem (T&BK). *Last known to nest at the Milford Twp. location in 1980. Prefers wooded
swamps, river and lake edges.

Yellow-crowned Night-Heron   *Nyctanassa violacea*
SUMMER VISITOR. RARE. Eight records, all since 1972. Early date: 4/16/79 (RMas). Late date: 8/8/72 (GAF). Most recent sighting: Martins Creek 8/3/91 (SBo). Prefers wooded swamps and lake edges.

Glossy Ibis   *Plegadis falcinellus*
VISITOR. RARE. Sightings increasing; most sightings in Spring. Early date: Wescosville 3/26/96 (JAF). Late date: Nockamixon State Park 9/15/91 (SF). High count: 11-Green Pond 3/30/98 (JH). One summer record: Nazareth 6/16/00 (RW). Found along ponds and in wet meadows.

Black Vulture   *Coragyps atratus*
RESIDENT. FAIRLY COMMON. First documented in 1974, this species has shown a steady increase in numbers and documented breeding in 1991. High count: 52-Unami Creek Valley 12/19/93 (GAF, GLF). Best found by watching for soaring birds along mountain ridges and wooded valleys, especially in the Unami Creek Valley.

Turkey Vulture   *Cathartes aura*
RESIDENT. COMMON. High count: 350-Unami Creek Valley 2/1/83 (GAF). Found soaring over most habitats.

Greater White-fronted Goose   *Anser albifrons*
WINTER VISITOR. RARE. Early date: Bake Oven Knob 10/12/71 (R&AMc). Late date: Green Lane Reservoir 3/19/77 (AM, RB). High count: 4-Green Lane Reservoir 3/13-18/94 (A&JM, mobs). Usually associated with Canada Goose.

Snow Goose   *Anser caerulescens*
MIGRANT, WINTER VISITOR. FAIRLY COMMON. Increase from sightings in the hundreds in the early- to mid-'80s, with a tremendous increase in the late 1990s, with early spring sightings of flocks numbering in the thousands. Early date: Green Lane Reservoir 9/24/98 (KFC). Late date: Upper Perkiomen Valley Park 5/22/00 (A&JM). High count: 10,000- Fogelsville Quarry mid-Feb. 1997 (mobs). Several summer records, most likely injured birds, unable to migrate. Found on lakes and quarries and in agricultural fields.

Ross's Goose   *Anser rossii*
MIGRANT, WINTER VISITOR. RARE. New to area. First documented: Fogelsville Quarry 2/16-21/97 (C & DM, mobs). Early date: Green Pond 11/16-12/3/98 (mobs). Late date: Green Pond 3/15-23/97 (DMi, JZ). High count: 3-Fogelsville Quarry 1/13/98 (JH, RW). Usually found with Snow Goose.

Canada Goose   *Branta canadensis*
RESIDENT. COMMON. High count: 28,000+ (in two hours) Baer Rocks 3/16/77 (MB). Numbers have increased dramatically since the '70s when this species was introduced as a breeding bird in Pennsylvania. Formerly a migrant, now common year-round and breeding near any body of water.

Brant   *Branta bernicla*
MIGRANT, WINTER VISITOR. RARE. Early date: Bake Oven Knob 9/12/68 (MB). Late date: Nockamixon State Park 5/24/96 (SF). High count: 1,560-Baer Rocks 10/13/74 (KK). Often associated with flocks of Canada Geese.

Mute Swan   *Cygnus olor*
RESIDENT. UNCOMMON. Feral birds have become resident at Minsi Lake, East Bangor Dam, and Lake Nockamixon. High count: 33-Lake Minsi 11/11/01 (RW).

Tundra Swan *Cygnus columbianus*
MIGRANT. UNCOMMON. Spring: Quakertown 2/3/90 (SF) – Green Lane Reservoir 4/18/01 (KFC). Fall: Nockamixon State Park 9/25/85 (SF) – 14-Green Lane Reservoir 12/21/96 (GAF). High count: 242-Baer Rocks 11/26/83 (KK). Most sightings from Feb. and March. Few winter records, usually during mild years.

Wood Duck *Aix sponsa*
RESIDENT. FAIRLY COMMON. Rare in winter. High count: 108-Upper Black Eddy 9/27/92 (SF). Found along wooded shorelines of lakes, rivers, and streams. Most often found at East Bangor Dam and Upper Perkiomen Valley Park.

Gadwall *Anas strepera*
MIGRANT, WINTER VISITOR. UNCOMMON. Early date: 9/20/80 (GAF). Late date: Green Pond 5/7/99 (RW). High count: 60-Upper Perkiomen Valley Park 11/10/91 (KFC). Found on lakes and ponds, generally preferring more sheltered areas.

Eurasian Wigeon *Anas penelope*
CASUAL. First recorded at Lake Muhlenberg 11/12/55-1/2/56 (CM, JT). Reported at Lake Muhlenberg during the winters from 1963-1973.

American Wigeon *Anas americana*
MIGRANT, WINTER VISITOR. UNCOMMON. Early date: Green Lane Reservoir 8/23/98 (A&JM). Late date: 5/24/80 (GAF). One summer record: Upper Perkiomen Valley Park 6/17 – 7/25/90 (MMc, mobs.) High count: 70-Green Lane Reservoir 3/13/01 (KFC). Found on lakes and ponds, generally preferring more sheltered areas.

American Black Duck *Anas rubripes*
YEAR-ROUND VISITOR. COMMON in winter, rare and local in summer. Breeding status unknown. High count: 450-Martins Creek Quarry 12/4/95 (BHo). Found on lakes and larger impoundments.

Mallard *Anas platyrhynchos*
RESIDENT. COMMON. Found on most bodies of water.

Blue-winged Teal *Anas discors*
MIGRANT. UNCOMMON. Spring: Green Lane Reservoir 3/6/88 (KFC) – Green Lane Reservoir 5/16/92 (KFC). Fall: Spring Creek 7/31/89 (RW) - 11/12/79 (KK). High count: 52-Minsi Lake 9/7/78 (RW). Four winter records and a few summer records. Found on lakes and ponds, generally preferring more sheltered areas.

Northern Shoveler *Anas clypeata*
MIGRANT, WINTER VISITOR. UNCOMMON. Early date: Green Lane Reservoir 7/29/87 (GLF). Late date: 5/15/73 (RW, WW). High count: 38-Green Lane Reservoir 10/8/98 (KFC). At least one summer record: Green Lane Reservoir 6/15/91 (GLF). Found on lakes and ponds, generally preferring more sheltered areas.

Northern Pintail *Anas acuta*
MIGRANT, WINTER VISITOR. FAIRLY COMMON. Early date: Martins Creek 8/30/95 (RW). Late date: Minsi Lake 5/17/92 (SBo). High count: 651-Green Lane Reservoir 3/21/81 (GAF). One summer record: Green Lane Reservoir 6/13/91 (RG). Found on lakes and larger impoundments.

Green-winged Teal *Anas crecca*
MIGRANT, WINTER VISITOR. FAIRLY COMMON. Early date: Green Lane Reservoir 7/21/88 (RW). Late date: Green Pond 5/31/98 (RW). High count: 350+ Green Lane Reservoir 10/23/99 (GAF). A number of summer records. Found on lakes and ponds, preferring areas with emergent vegetation.

Canvasback *Aythya valisineria*
MIGRANT, WINTER VISITOR. RARE. Early date: 10/7/79 (KK). Late date: 4/17/81 (GLF). High count: 29-Dorney Park Pond 2/25/77 (RW). Sightings have declined considerably in recent years. Found on lakes and larger impoundments.

Redhead *Aythya americana*
MIGRANT, WINTER VISITOR. RARE. Early date: Upper Perkiomen Valley Park 10/4/96 (KFC). Late date: 5/13/81 (T&BK). High count: 37-Chain Dam 3/9/78 (WW, RW). Sightings have declined considerably in recent years. Possible on most bodies of water.

Ring-necked Duck *Aythya collaris*
MIGRANT, WINTER VISITOR. COMMON. Early date: 9/13/80 (BLM). Late date: Green Pond 6/5/98 (RW). High count: 400-Albert Road Ponds 3/19/01 (RW). At least four summer records. Found on lakes and ponds.

Greater Scaup *Aythya marila*
MIGRANT, WINTER VISITOR. RARE. Early date: 10/10/79 (BLM). Late date: Green Lane Reservoir 5/24/87 (KFC). High count: 22-Nockamixon State Park 3/17/01 (A&JM, DF). One summer record: Allentown 6/6-9/97 (AJ). Usually found on larger lakes and reservoirs.

Lesser Scaup *Aythya affinis*
MIGRANT, WINTER VISITOR. UNCOMMON. Early date: 9/26/53 (CB). Late date: Martins Creek 5/22/00 (RW). High count: 70-Beltzville State Park 11/28/81 (RW, BSi). Four summer records. Usually found on larger lakes and reservoirs.

Surf Scoter *Melanitta perspicillata*
MIGRANT, WINTER VISITOR. RARE. At least 11 area records. First recorded 1/2/68 Fish Hatchery (EMas -specimen). Early date: Leaser Lake 10/19/96 (KD, RW). Late date: Beltzville State Park 5/10/88 (RW). High count: 8-Wild Creek Reservoir 11/19/82 (JG). Usually found on larger lakes and reservoirs.

White-winged Scoter *Melanitta fusca*
MIGRANT, WINTER VISITOR. RARE. Early date: 10/14/78 (RW). Late date: Nockamixon State Park 5/22/97 (SF). High count: 63-Beltzville State Park 10/29/84 (BR). This is the most frequently reported of the three scoter species. Usually found on larger lakes and reservoirs.

Black Scoter *Melanitta nigra*
FALL MIGRANT. RARE. Early date: 10/13/74 (RW). Late date: 11/18/84 (KS). When present, this scoter species is usually found in large numbers; typically 20-50 individuals. High count: 500-Green Lane Reservoir 10/23/77 (GAF). All sightings from Oct. & Nov., except for two sightings: Leaser Lake 1/24-26/99 (MMo, mobs) and Minsi Lake 4/11/01 (RW). Usually found on larger lakes and reservoirs.

Long-tailed Duck (Oldsquaw) *Clangula hyemalis*
MIGRANT. RARE. Spring: Green Lane Reservoir 3/13/92 (NT) - Beltzville State Park 4/30/90 (RW). Fall: Beltzville State Park 10/23/93 (RW) – Green Lane Reservoir 11/25/99 (KFC). High count: 96-Nockamixon State Park 4/2/93 (SF). Three winter records: Whitehall 12/26/70 (DW, RW), Penn Forest Reservoir 1/8/86 (RW, SBo, GY), and Beltzville State Park 1/3/91 (RW). Usually found on larger lakes and reservoirs.

Bufflehead *Bucephala albeola*
MIGRANT, WINTER VISITOR. FAIRLY COMMON. Early date: 10/17/82 (GLF). Late date: 5/24/78 (RW). High count: 130-Beltzville State Park 4/14/96 (DHa). Three summer records: Dorney Pond 5/31-6/17/77 (RW-photo), Leaser Lake 6/15/80 (KK), and Martins Creek 8/3/00 (SBo, mobs). Usually found on larger lakes, reservoirs, and rivers.

Common Goldeneye *Bucephala clangula*
MIGRANT, WINTER VISITOR. UNCOMMON. Early date: 10/29/83 (BLM). Late date: Green Lane Reservoir 5/3/97 (KFC). High count: 210-Merrill Creek Reservoir 2/13/00 (RW). Found on larger lakes, reservoirs, and rivers.

Barrow's Goldeneye *Bucephala islandica*
ACCIDENTAL. New to area. One record: One male and two females at Merrill Creek Reservoir 2/16-27/00 (DDu, RW-photo, mobs). These birds moved between Merrill Creek Reservoir and the Delaware River at Foul Rift. In addition, one male, believed to be a Barrow's X Common Goldeneye hybrid, was seen on the Delaware River at Portland 2/26/00 (RW, SBo).

Hooded Merganser *Lophodytes cucullatus*
MIGRANT, WINTER VISITOR. UNCOMMON. Early date: 8/27/79 (RW). Late date: Green Lane Reservoir 5/31/93 (GLF). High count: 37-Upper Perkiomen Valley Park 12/28/01 (KFC). Found along the edges of lakes, wooded streams, and rivers.

Common Merganser *Mergus merganser*
RESIDENT. FAIRLY COMMON. Most abundant during spring migration. Uncommon in summer, with a small breeding population along Delaware River. Other summer records from Wild Creek & Penn Forest Reservoirs, and the upper Lehigh River. High count: 1,236-Nockamixon State Park 3/10/01 (AM). Found on larger lakes and rivers.

Red-breasted Merganser *Mergus serrator*
MIGRANT, WINTER VISITOR. UNCOMMON. Early date: Bake Oven Knob 9/18/71 (DH). Late date: Hecktown 5/24/78 (RW). High count: 45-Beltzville State Park 4/13/95 (PBS). Three summer records: Leaser Lake 7/10/84 (SS), Penn Forest Reservoir 6/26/93 (RW), and Martins Creek 7/30/95 (DDe, BH, RW). Found on larger lakes and rivers.

Ruddy Duck *Oxyura jamaicensis*
MIGRANT. UNCOMMON. Spring: Nockamixon State Park 3/11/01 (A&JM) – Martins Creek 5/24/00 (RW). Fall: Dorney Landfill 9/1/01 (B&PM) - Green Lane Reservoir 12/16/01 (RG, LRh). High count: 267-Green Lane Reservoir 10/31/99 (GAF). Four summer records and a few winter records. Found on larger lakes and rivers.

Osprey *Pandion haliaetus*
BREEDING BIRD. FAIRLY COMMON. Most sightings during migration. Reintroduced breeding bird. Early date: Revere 3/1/90 (SF). Late date: Nockamixon State Park 11/29/91 (KFC). High count: 171-Baer Rocks 4/14/90 (KK). Four area Christmas Count records, and one January record: Beltzville State Park 1/19/88 (DBe, AKr). Five nests in Northampton Co in 1998 (TM). Found at lakes, reservoirs, and larger rivers.

Swallow-tailed Kite *Elanoides forficatus*
ACCIDENTAL. Two records: Allentown 5/35 (CM, CR) and Jonas 5/24/91 (RZ). Possible in most rural habitats.

Mississippi Kite *Ictinia mississippiensis*
CASUAL. New to area. At least six records. First record: Scott's Mt. 5/4/86 (GH). Additional records: Morgan's Hill 4/23/88 (DDe, mobs), Morgan's Hill 4/4/91 (AK, AL), Morgan's Hill 4/20/92 (AK), Williams Twp. 4/18/01 (AK), and Nockamixon Twp. 5/28/01 (DF-photo, under review). Possible in most rural habitats.

Bald Eagle *Haliaeetus leucocephalus*
RESIDENT. UNCOMMON. High count: 16-Little Gap Bird Observatory 9/17/99 (MS, AMi, KMi). Only known breeding location is Merrill Creek Reservoir. Sightings increasing at area reservoirs and along the Delaware River.

Northern Harrier *Circus cyaneus*
MIGRANT, WINTER VISITOR. UNCOMMON. Early date: Jacobsburg State Park 8/2/96 (RW). Late date: Unami Creek Valley 5/23/98 (GAF). High count: 62-Bake Oven Knob 10/28/74 (R&AMc). Two summer records: New Tripoli 7/27/90 (JG, DG) and Kesslersville 7/4/96 (RW, JFe, JHof). Prefers large open marshes and fields.

Sharp-shinned Hawk *Accipiter striatus*
YEAR-ROUND VISITOR. COMMON during fall migration, uncommon to rare in other seasons. High count: 1,437-Baer Rocks 10/2/77 (KK). Found along edges of woods and often hunts around bird feeders.

Cooper's Hawk *Accipiter cooperii*
RESIDENT. FAIRLY COMMON. Most abundant during fall migration, uncommon in other seasons. High count: 186-Baer Rocks 10/8/81 (KK). Found along edges of woods and often hunts around bird feeders.

Northern Goshawk *Accipiter gentilis*
MIGRANT, WINTER VISITOR. UNCOMMON. Uncommon during fall migration, rare in other seasons. Only known breeding record was in 1986 at Wild Creek Reservoir (RW). High count: 35-Bake Oven Knob 11/3/72 (KK). Found in extensive mature forest, and along the Kittatinny Ridge during migration.

Red-shouldered Hawk *Buteo lineatus*
YEAR-ROUND VISITOR. UNCOMMON and declining. Former Breeding Bird. Most sightings during fall migration. High count: 69-Bake Oven Knob 10/30/68 (R&AMc). Prefers mature moist forest and wooded swamps.

Broad-winged Hawk *Buteo platypterus*
BREEDING BIRD. COMMON. Most common during fall migration, uncommon breeder. Early date: Emmaus 3/12/90 (JH). Late date: 11/17/84 (FB). High count: 18,500-Scott's Mt. 9/14/83 (GH, mobs). Found in mature forests, and along ridges during migration.

Swainson's Hawk *Buteo swainsoni*
CASUAL. 13 area reports since 1978, all in fall. Early date: Bake Oven Knob 9/11/86 (RB, DH). Late date: Bake Oven Knob 11/12/89 (FB, AK). Extreme caution should be used when trying to separate this species from other buteos. According to McWilliams and Brauning (2000), "Hawk-watch reports suggests that they are regular in Pennsylvania, but there is a lack of documentation for this species."

Red-tailed Hawk *Buteo jamaicensis*
RESIDENT. COMMON. High count: 914-Bake Oven Knob 11/13/82 (GLF, mobs). This species has shown a steady increase over the last 20 years and can be found in nearly any habitat type, including suburban settings.

Rough-legged Hawk *Buteo lagopus*
MIGRANT, WINTER VISITOR. RARE and Irruptive. Early date: 10/3/74 (KK). Late date: 4/30/72 (KK). High count: 13 near Beltzville 1/20/79 (BLM). Found in large open fields, and along the Kittatinny Ridge during migration.

Golden Eagle *Aquila chrysaetos*
MIGRANT. UNCOMMON. Spring: Green Lane Reservoir 3/31/01 (JHo) – 5/1/74 (GAF). Fall: 9/9/75 (DH) – Unknown. High count: 13-Bake Oven Knob 11/11/87 (RW). A few winter records. Found mainly along the Kittatinny Ridge during migration.

American Kestrel *Falco sparverius*
RESIDENT. FAIRLY COMMON. High count: 154-Baer Rocks 4/2/74 (KK). Found mainly in open country along roads perched on wires.

Merlin *Falco columbarius*
MIGRANT, WINTER VISITOR. UNCOMMON. Early date: Beltzville State Park 8/9/99 (JH, RW). Late date: Little Gap 5/19/99 (BSi, JSi). High count: 51- Baer Rocks 10/22/89 (TKl). Edges of woods, field edges, and along ridges during migration.

Gyrfalcon *Falco rusticolus*
CASUAL. At least 16 reported sightings. Most sightings in fall from hawk watch sites. Last record: Merrill Creek Reservoir 1/2/01 (JB). According to McWilliams and Brauning (2000) "it is likely that a few Peregrine Falcons are misidentified as Gyrfalcons." Edges of woods, field edges, quarries, and along ridges during migration.

Peregrine Falcon *Falco peregrinus*
MIGRANT. UNCOMMON. Spring: Martins Creek 3/18/00 (RW) – 5/15/84 (EW). Fall: Green Lane Reservoir 8/2/00 (KFC) – Little Gap 11/12/90 (MSc). High count: 10-Bake Oven Knob 10/6/87 (BHi, RHi, KK). One December record: Monocacy Nature Center 12/11/00 (RW, mobs). Edges of woods, field edges, quarries, and along ridges during migration.

Ring-necked Pheasant *Phasianus colchicus*
RESIDENT. RARE. Formerly common, now rare due to changes in agricultural practices and habitat loss. Wild populations periodically augmented by restocking programs. Found in agricultural fields and meadows with dense brush nearby.

Ruffed Grouse *Bonasa umbellus*
RESIDENT. UNCOMMON. Population stable along the Kittatinny Ridge and in the Wild Creek & Penn Forest Reservoir areas. Mostly absent from southern portion of area. Found in mature deciduous and mixed forest.

Wild Turkey *Meleagris gallopavo*
RESIDENT. FAIRLY COMMON. Reintroduction programs very successful. Flocks of 100+ seen in some areas. Found in mature deciduous forest; also feeds in agricultural fields.

Northern Bobwhite *Colinus virginianus*
EXTIRPATED. Former Resident. Current sightings are of released individuals, having little chance of becoming established. Found in brushy, overgrown fields and along the edges of agricultural areas.

Yellow Rail *Coturnicops noveboracensis*
ACCIDENTAL. One record: 5/14/50 at Lake Warren, Bucks Co. (ABr, R&LT in Thomas 1953). One recent report Williams Twp. 10/31/01 (AK, under review). Prefers wet, grassy fields.

King Rail *Rallus elegans*
ACCIDENTAL. One record: 5/9/54 Alburtis (CM, mobs). One additional unconfirmed heard only record in the '80s at Quakertown Swamp (HR). Found in marshes and swamps.

Virginia Rail *Rallus limicola*
MIGRANT, BREEDING BIRD. Rare. Early date: Quakertown Swamp 4/8/01 (DF). Late date: Quakertown Swamp 12/21/74 (J&EP, mobs). High count: 12-Quakertown Swamp 5/3/87 (GAF). Found in densely vegetated swamps and marshes.

Sora *Porzana carolina*
MIGRANT, BREEDING BIRD. RARE. Early date: Green Lane Reservoir 3/15/86 (JH). Late date: 10/7/78 (D&EM). Prefers densely vegetated swamps and marshes.

Purple Gallinule *Porphyrula martinica*
ACCIDENTAL. 2 records: 6/20/77 at Easton (MM-specimen, in Paxton et al. 1977 and 6/4-9/85 Lake Warren, (SF, HR, BB). Found in marshes and swamps.

Common Moorhen *Gallinula chloropus*
MIGRANT, SUMMER VISITOR. RARE. Early date: Green Lane Reservoir 4/17/92 (G&KC). Late date: Upper Perkiomen Valley Park 10/27/91 (KFC, mobs). High count: 2-Green Lane Reservoir 5/9-11/95 (RB, KFC, mobs). One winter record: Bushkill Creek 12/31/65 (WC-photo). Found at ponds and lakes with dense vegetation along banks.

American Coot *Fulica americana*
YEAR-ROUND VISITOR. UNCOMMON. Rare in summer. High count: 95-Nockamixon State Park 2/17/95 (A&JM). Found at lakes and larger ponds.

Sandhill Crane *Grus canadensis*
MIGRANT, WINTER VISITOR. RARE. At least 12 records. Early date: Green Lane Reservoir 10/6/94 (JPu, mobs). Late date: (high count) 6-Bally 5/16/92 (H&EH). One summer record: 7/14/95 (AK). Found most often near water and in wet meadows.

Black-bellied Plover *Pluvialis squatarola*
MIGRANT. UNCOMMON. Spring: Martins Creek 4/27/00 (RW) – Green Pond 6/4/98 (RW). Fall: 8/3/84 (DHe) – Green Lane Reservoir 11/16/91 (KFC). High count: 18-Cherry Hill 10/12/75 (WC). Found on mud flats and in wet fields.

American Golden-Plover *Pluvialis dominica*
MIGRANT. RARE. Spring: Spring Creek 3/22/78 (SS) – Phillipsburg 4/16/83 (GH). Fall: 7/24/85 (BLM) – Green Lane Reservoir 11/20/78 (RW). High count: 108-Fogelsville 8/23/94 (RW). Found on mud flats and in wet fields.

Semipalmated Plover *Charadrius semipalmatus*
MIGRANT. UNCOMMON. Spring: Green Lane Reservoir 4/22/94 (KKn) – Bath 6/9/90 (RW). Fall: Green Lane Reservoir 7/17/99 (A&JM) – Green Lane Reservoir 11/17/88 (FBa). High count: 42-Green Lane Reservoir 8/12/98 (KFC). Found on mud flats and in wet fields.

Killdeer *Charadrius vociferus*
RESIDENT. COMMON. Rare in winter. High count: 175-Martins Creek 11/3/95 (RW). Found in pastures, meadows, and on mud flats.

American Oystercatcher *Haematopus palliatus*
ACCIDENTAL. New to area. One record: Beltzville State Park 4/02/93 (RW-photo).

Black-necked Stilt *Himantopus mexicanus*
ACCIDENTAL. One record: 5/12/81 at Nazareth Sewage Ponds (BK-photo, mobs). Prefers mud flats and edges of lakes and ponds.

American Avocet *Recurvirostra americana*
CASUAL. New to area. 7 records. First record: Green Lane Reservoir 11/3-9/91 (GAF, mobs). Early date: Green Lane Reservoir 7/15/00 (RB, GAF). Late date: Schantz Road, Allentown 11/11-17/91 (DK, mobs). High count: 2-Green Lane Reservoir 9/11-18/98 (KFC-photo, mobs). Found on mud flats and in wet fields.

Greater Yellowlegs *Tringa melanoleuca*
MIGRANT. FAIRLY COMMON. Spring: Green Lane Reservoir 3/19/83 (GLF) – 6/5/78 (mobs). Fall: Green Lane Reservoir 7/7/80 (GLF) – Green Lane Reservoir 11/8/81 (GLF). High count: 15-Green Lane Reservoir 8/12/97 (KFC). Found on mud flats and in wet fields.

Lesser Yellowlegs *Tringa flavipes*
MIGRANT. COMMON. Spring: Green Lane Reservoir 3/14/82 (GLF) – 6/2/82 (SS). Fall: Green Lane Reservoir 6/30/99 (GAF) – Green Lane Reservoir 11/16/91 (KFC). High count: 150-Green Lane Reservoir 9/2/81 (GAF). Found on mud flats and in wet fields.

Solitary Sandpiper *Tringa solitaria*
MIGRANT. FAIRLY COMMON. Spring: East Bangor Dam 4/4/91 (DDe) – 6/3/84 (FB). Fall: Green Pond 7/2/98 (RW) – Jordan Creek Parkway 10/25/89 (TFr). High count: 38-Fogelsville 5/3/83 (BLM, SS). Usually found along edges of ponds, lakes, and streams.

Willet *Catoptrophorus semipalmatus*
CASUAL. Five records: Bangor 5/9/71 (DE), Green Lane Reservoir 9/76 (RB), Catasauqua 8/78 (AR), Minsi Lake 5/7/84 (SBo, BSi-photo), and 2-Martins Creek 7/23/96 (RW-photo). Found on mud flats and in wet fields.

Spotted Sandpiper *Actitis macularia*
BREEDING BIRD. COMMON. Early date: Green Lane Reservoir 4/9/99 (KFC). Late date: 10/21/78 (BLM). High count: 37-Minsi Lake 5/24/97 (BSi, JSi). Usually found along edges of ponds, lakes, rivers, and streams.

Upland Sandpiper *Bartramia longicauda*
MIGRANT. RARE and declining. Former Breeding Bird; a few recent summer records, but breeding status unknown. Early date: 4/20/81 (BK). Late date: 10/27/79 (GH). High count: 22-LVI Airport 8/4/92 (RW). Prefers large hay and grass fields; also large turf areas at airports.

Whimbrel *Numenius phaeopus*
CASUAL. New to area. Three records: 30-Scott's Mt. 9/7/86 (JE, GH), Macungie 8/1/88 (RW), and 2-Nockamixon State Park 4/23/00 (DF, JH, under review). Found on mud flats and in wet fields.

Hudsonian Godwit *Limosa haemastica*
CASUAL. Nine records, all in fall. Seven records from Green Lane Reservior. Early date (and high count): 4-Martins Creek 8/17/98 (RW). Late date: Green Lane Reservoir 10/13-11/20/97 (KFC, mobs). Found on mud flats and in wet fields.

Ruddy Turnstone *Arenaria interpres*
MIGRANT. RARE. Spring: Beltzville State Park 5/9/92 (BSi, RW) – Fogelsville 5/17/94 (RW). Fall: Green Lane Reservoir 7/26/85 (BLM, GLF) – Baer Rocks 10/7/79 (KK). High count: 1,500-Green Lane Reservoir 6/4/00 (DF). Found on mud flats and edges of lakes.

Red Knot *Calidris canutus*
MIGRANT. RARE. Spring: Emmaus 5/7/84 (KB) – 300-Green Lane Reservoir 5/28/99 (DF-photo, JH, mobs). Fall: Green Lane Reservoir 9/6/81 (BSi, RW, mobs) – Bake Oven Knob 9/24/79 (FM). Found on mud flats at lakes and reservoirs.

Sanderling *Calidris alba*
MIGRANT. RARE. Spring: Nazareth Sewage Ponds 4/28/79 (GH) – Beltzville State Park 5/31/92 (JH, B&PM). Fall: Green Lane Reservoir 7/31/98 (KFC) – Green Lane Reservoir 11/8/97 (GAF, GLF, LRh, KFC). High count: 4-Beltzville State Park 8/24/90 (RW). Found on mud flats at lakes and reservoirs.

Semipalmated Sandpiper *Calidris pusilla*
MIGRANT. FAIRLY COMMON. Spring: 5/3/80 (WC) – Green Lane Reservoir 6/10/93 (KFC). Fall: Green Lane Reservoir 7/15/00 (A&JM) – Green Lane Reservoir 11/17/91 (FBa). High count: 100-Green Lane Reservoir 7/31/98 (GAF). Found on mud flats at lakes and reservoirs.

Western Sandpiper *Calidris mauri*
MIGRANT. UNCOMMON. Spring: 5/9/79 (SS) – 5/23/81 (WC). Fall: 7/16/81 (SS) – Green Lane Reservoir 11/17/91 (FBa). High count: 17-Nazareth Sewage Ponds 5/11/82 (WC). Found on mud flats at lakes and reservoirs.

Least Sandpiper *Calidris minutilla*
MIGRANT. COMMON. Spring: Green Lane Reservoir 4/21/95 (KFC) – 6/3/79 (BK, D&EM). Fall: Green Lane Reservoir 6/29/88 (GAF) – 11/20/78 (SS, RW). High count: 225-Green Lane Reservoir 8/12/99 (A&JM). One winter record: Dorney Pond 12/17-20/88 (BT). Found on mud flats at lakes and reservoirs.

White-rumped Sandpiper *Calidris fuscicollis*
MIGRANT. UNCOMMON. Spring: Green Lane Reservoir 5/1/82 (GAF) – Point Phillips 6/3/90 (DDe, BW). Fall: Green Lane Reservoir 7/19/80 (GLF) – Green Lane Reservoir 11/20/91 (RW). High count: 16-Green Lane Reservoir 11/14/91 (KFC, RW). Found on mud flats at lakes and reservoirs.

Baird's Sandpiper *Calidris bairdii*
FALL MIGRANT. RARE. Green Lane Reservoir 7/19/97 (KFC) – Green Lane Reservoir 11/11/78 (RW). High count: 8-Green Lane Reservoir 8/8/87 (RW). Found on mud flats at lakes and reservoirs.

Pectoral Sandpiper *Calidris melanotos*
MIGRANT. UNCOMMON. Spring: Klecknersville 3/15/91 (DDe) – 5/23/81 (WC). Fall: Green Lane Reservoir 7/7/80 (GLF) – 12/2/78 (SS). High count: 170-Green Lane Reservoir 9/2/81 (GLF). Found on mud flats at lakes and reservoirs.

Dunlin *Calidris alpina*
MIGRANT. UNCOMMON. Spring: Nockamixon State Park 4/4/00 (DF, A&JM) – Martins Creek 6/3/99 (RW). Fall: Green Lane Reservoir 8/1/93 (GAF) – Green Lane Reservoir 11/18/00 (KFC). High count: 37-Green Lane Reservoir 11/1/81 (RG). Found on mud flats at lakes and reservoirs.

Stilt Sandpiper *Calidris himantopus*
FALL MIGRANT. UNCOMMON. Green Lane Reservoir 7/14/99 (A&JM) – Green Lane Reservoir 11/2/01 (AM). High count: 48-Green Lane Reservoir 9/2/81 (mobs). Found on mud flats at lakes and reservoirs.

Buff-breasted Sandpiper   *Tryngites subruficollis*
FALL MIGRANT. RARE. Fogelsville 8/24/94 (RW) – 9/22/83 (BLM). High count: 4-Green Lane Reservoir 9/18/80 (GLF). Found on mud flats at lakes and reservoirs, as well as temporary ponds in fields.

Ruff   *Philomachus pugnax*
ACCIDENTAL. Two sightings: Spring Creek 5/14-15/83 (SS-photo, BLM, mobs) and Green Lane Reservoir 9/14/83 (GLF, MS). Found on mud flats and in shallow flooded fields.

Short-billed Dowitcher   *Limnodromus griseus*
MIGRANT. UNCOMMON. Spring: 4/2/78 (SS) – Green Lane Reservoir 5/29/92 (GAF, KFC). Fall: Green Lane Reservoir 7/2/81 (GLF) – 10/27/79 (BK). High count: 53-Green Lane Reservoir 5/19/87 (RW). Found on mud flats at lakes and reservoirs.

Long-billed Dowitcher   *Limnodromus scolopaceus*
FALL MIGRANT. RARE. Early date: Spring Creek 7/22/84 (BLM) – Green Lane Reservoir 11/3-16/91 (RW, mobs). High count: 3-Green Lane Reservoir 8/3/74 (GAF). Found on mud flats at lakes and reservoirs.

Common Snipe   *Gallinago gallinago*
MIGRANT, WINTER VISITOR. UNCOMMON. Rare to absent in winter. Early date: 8/2/84 (SBo, RW). Late date: 5/15/88 (KS, AK). High count: 50+ Hecktown 4/1/79 (SBo). Two summer records: Williams Twp. 6/2/82 (AK) and Harmony Twp. 7/16/76 (JE). Found in marshes, meadows, and occasionally on mud flats.

American Woodcock   *Scolopax minor*
BREEDING BIRD. UNCOMMON. Early date: Revere 2/11/98 (SF). Late Date: Henningsville 12/19/92 (DK, PGS). A few winter records. Most often heard on spring evenings when males are displaying. Prefers wet second growth forest, small clearings, and meadows.

Wilson's Phalarope   *Phalaropus tricolor*
MIGRANT. RARE. Spring: 5/6/78 (GH) – Green Pond 6/6/98 (JZ). Fall: Green Lane Reservoir 7/28/95 (KFC, JH) – 9/8/83 (GLF). High count: 4-Spring Creek 8/3/84 (SS). Usually found in shallow water along mud flats and flooded fields.

Red-necked Phalarope   *Phalaropus lobatus*
MIGRANT. RARE. Spring: 5/7/54 (CB, RMan) – 5/26/80 (LK-photo, mobs). Fall: 8/15/77 (RW) – Green Lane Reservoir 10/12/88 (RW-photo). High count: 7-Green Lane Reservoir 8/25/81 (mobs). Usually found in shallow water along mud flats and flooded fields.

Red Phalarope   *Phalaropus fulicaria*
ACCIDENTAL. Three records: Green Lane Reservoir 9/30/72 (C & DM), Green Lane Reservoir 11/3-4/80 (RW-photo, mobs) and Green Lane Reservoir 9/20/91 (GAF, RG). Usually found in shallow water along mud flats and flooded fields.

Laughing Gull   *Larus atricilla*
VISITOR. RARE. Most sightings in spring and fall. Early date: Nockamixon State Park 4/12/01 (BE). Late date: Green Lane Reservoir 11/26/92 (RG). High count: 2-Green Lane Reservoir 7/25/85 (RW). Found at larger lakes and reservoirs.

Little Gull   *Larus minutus*
ACCIDENTAL. New to area. Three known records: An adult bird at Merrill Creek Reservoir 4/5/00 (RDu) and two additional sightings (both under review), an adult at Martins Creek 4/7/01 (RW), and one at Nockamixon State Park 4/12/01 (BE). Found at larger lakes and reservoirs, usually with Bonaparte's Gulls.

Bonaparte's Gull *Larus philadelphia*
MIGRANT, WINTER VISITOR. UNCOMMON. Early date: Beltzville State Park 9/26/83 (RW). Late date: Leaser Lake 5/21/88 (FB, JZ, mobs). High count: 300-Beltzville State Park 4/13/87 (RW). Three summer records: Beltzville State Park 8/11/89 (RW), Nockamixon State Park 7/19/96 (IB), and Beltzville State Park 8/13/99 (RW). Found at lakes, rivers, and flooded fields.

Ring-billed Gull *Larus delawarensis*
YEAR-ROUND VISITOR. COMMON in winter and rare in summer. High count: 8,000-Green Lane Reservoir 3/24/84 (GAF, GLF). Found at lakes, rivers, agricultural fields, and landfills.

Herring Gull *Larus argentatus*
WINTER VISITOR. COMMON. Early date: Beltzville State Park 8/10/90 (RW). Late date: 5/25/79 (DC, RB). High count: 500-Easton 12/25/79 (GH). Three summer records: 7/4/90 (BLM, PE), Allentown 7/21/91 (BLM), and Beltzville State Park 7/19/93 (RW). Found at lakes, rivers, and landfills.

Iceland Gull *Larus glaucoides*
WINTER VISITOR. RARE. New to area. First record: 1/12/92 (AK, FB). Early date: Green Lane Reservoir 1/4/98 (KFC). Late date: Nockamixon State Park 4/12/94 (SF). High count: 2-Chain Dam, Easton 1/6/99 (RW, mobs). Found at lakes, rivers, and landfills.

Lesser Black-backed Gull *Larus fuscus*
WINTER VISITOR. UNCOMMON. New to area. Sightings increasing. First reported: Martins Creek 11/16/83 (SBo). Early date: Martins Creek 9/14/00 (RW). Late date: Nockamixon State Park 5/16/01 (A&JM). High count: 30-Nockamixon State Park 3/29/01 (BE). Found at lakes, rivers, and landfills.

Glaucous Gull *Larus hyperboreus*
CASUAL. Seven records: Green Lane Reservoir 3/23 - 4/29/78 (RB, DC), Nockamixon State Park 2/20/90 (ABr-photo, SF), Merrill Creek Reservoir 1/6/94 (RW), Green Lane Reservoir 1/20/99 (GAF), 3-(high count) Chain Dam, Easton 1/99 (DDe-photo, RW), Martins Creek 2/29/00 (RW), and Easton 12/1-2/00 (A&JM, mobs). Found at lakes, rivers, and landfills.

Great Black-backed Gull *Larus marinus*
WINTER VISITOR. FAIRLY COMMON. Early date: Nockamixon State Park 9/16/01 (BE). Late date: Nockamixon State Park 5/22/01 (A&JM). High count: 100+ Nockamixon State Park 4/90 (SF). Three summer records: Green Lane Reservoir 6/30/94 (GLF), Martins Creek 7/25/01 (RW), and a first year bird seen along the Delaware River near Easton 8/11-31/01 (DB, DDe). Found at lakes, rivers, and landfills.

Sabine's Gull *Xema sabini*
ACCIDENTAL. New to area. One record: A juvenile at Merrill Creek Reservoir 10/8-15/00 (RKa, mobs, RW-photo).

Caspian Tern *Sterna caspia*
MIGRANT. UNCOMMON. Sightings increasing. Spring: Green Lane Reservoir 4/4/00 (KFC, JH) – Beltzville State Park 5/31/92 (PE, JH, BLM). Fall: Green Lane Reservoir 7/22/97 (KFC) – Scott's Mt. 11/5/80 (GH). High count: 21-Green Lane Reservoir 8/29/99 (GAF, RK, KR). A few summer records. Found at larger lakes and rivers.

Common Tern *Sterna hirundo*
MIGRANT. RARE. Spring: Nockamixon State Park 4/13/01 (AM, DF, mobs) – Beltzville State Park 5/31/92 (PE, JH, BLM). Fall: Green Lane Reservoir 7/29/00 (KFC) – Beltzville State Park 11/17/78 (BLM, BSi, RW). High count: 5-Beltzville State Park 5/5/90 (RW). Two summer records: Nockamixon State Park 7/5/80 (BK), 2-Beltzville State Park 6/7/89 (RW). Found at larger lakes.

Arctic Tern *Sterna paradisaea*
ACCIDENTAL. New to area. One record: 2 at Beltzville State Park 5/16/89 (RW-photo).

Forster's Tern *Sterna forsteri*
MIGRANT. RARE. Spring: Green Lane Reservoir 4/11/83 (GLF) – Beltzville State Park 6/15/91 (SBo). Fall: Green Lane Reservoir 7/21/93 (KFC, GAF) – Green Lane Reservoir 10/27/86 (KFC). High count: 12-Beltzville State Park 5/10/89 (RW). One summer record: Green Lane Reservoir 7/2/91 (GAF, GLF). Found at larger lakes.

Least Tern *Sterna antillarum*
CASUAL. Four records. Bethlehem 8/30/60 (CB, WT, mobs), Green Lane Reservoir 6/24/93 (GLF, JH), Green Lane Reservoir 7/25/97 (JH, C&DM), and 2-Green Lane Reservoir 7/14/99 (AM). Found at larger lakes.

Black Tern *Chlidonias niger*
MIGRANT. RARE. Spring: Beltzville State Park 5/2/89 (RW) – Minsi Lake 6/3/96 (RW). Fall: Green Lane Reservoir 8/2/93 (RW) – Minsi Lake 10/30/75 (CM). High count: 12-Green Lane Reservoir 8/14/94 (GAF). Found at larger lakes and marshes.

Dovekie *Alle alle*
ACCIDENTAL. Two records: Lehigh River, Allentown Feb. 1924 (JT) and Bethlehem 11/12/70 (EMa-specimen).

Rock Dove *Columba livia*
RESIDENT. COMMON. Found in cities, towns, and agricultural areas.

Mourning Dove *Zenaida macroura*
RESIDENT. COMMON. Found in farmland and suburbs.

Black-billed Cuckoo *Coccyzus erythropthalmus*
BREEDING BIRD. UNCOMMON. Early date: 4/30/60 (CM). Late date: 10/14/74 (GH). Prefers mature and second growth forests.

Yellow-billed Cuckoo *Coccyzus americanus*
BREEDING BIRD. UNCOMMON. Early date: 4/22/84 (D&EM). Late date: 10/18/83 (BLM). Prefers mature and second growth forests.

Barn Owl *Tyto alba*
RESIDENT. RARE, LOCAL, and declining. Found hunting open fields and meadows.

Eastern Screech-Owl *Otus asio*
RESIDENT. COMMON. Prefers deciduous and mixed forests and woodlots.

Great Horned Owl *Bubo virginianus*
RESIDENT. COMMON. Found in forests and woodlots with mature trees; extremely adaptable.

Snowy Owl *Nyctea scandiaca*
WINTER VISITOR. IRRUPTIVE. Early date: 10/23/55 (MB). Late date: 4/6/92 (PE, mobs). High count: 2-LVI Airport January 1991 (mobs). Found in large open fields and turf areas of airports.

Barred Owl *Strix varia*
RESIDENT. UNCOMMON and local. Found most often in mature moist woods. Known to breed in the Wild Creek and Penn Forest Reservoirs area and in the Bear Swamp and Minsi Lake areas.

Great Gray Owl   *Strix nebulosa*
ACCIDENTAL. One record: A dead bird found 2/79 in a melting snow bank at Nockamixon State Park (FH-specimen).

Long-eared Owl   *Asio otus*
WINTER VISITOR. RARE. Early date: 11/29/92 (PE). Late date: Seemsville 4/2/94 (BM). High count: 25-Lynn Twp. 1/5/91 (FB, JH, B&PM). Found in coniferous forests and plantations.

Short-eared Owl   *Asio flammeus*
WINTER VISITOR. RARE AND IRRUPTIVE. Early date: Bake Oven Knob 10/23/89 (DG, JG). Late date: Morgan's Hill 4/22/90 (AK). High count: 7-Green Lane Reservoir 1/90 (GAF). Prefers open fields and meadows. Best found by watching these areas at dusk.

Northern Saw-whet Owl   *Aegolius acadicus*
RESIDENT. RARE. Occurs most often during migration, with a few birds wintering. Two documented breeding records: Revere 3/13-5/30/78 (SF) and a juvenile near Penn Forest Reservoir in summer 1985 (DBr). Difficult to find, prefers dense cover, especially evergreens.

Common Nighthawk   *Chordeiles minor*
BREEDING BIRD. FAIRLY COMMON. Early date: 2-Narazeth 2/21/92 (KS). Late date: 4-Allentown 11/18/93 (SF). High count: 290+ Allentown 8/22/82 (GH). Most easily seen or heard at dusk in urban areas where it nests on flat roof tops. During migration can also be seen hunting over any open area.

Whip-poor-will   *Caprimulgus vociferus*
BREEDING BIRD. UNCOMMON and declining. Early date: Wild Creek Reservoir 4/9/00 (BSi, JaSi). Late date: Revere 11/19/81 (SF). High count: 22-Penn Forest Reservoir 5/19/91 (DDe, SBo, BSi, RW). Found in second growth forests, from Kittatinny Ridge and north.

Chimney Swift   *Chaetura pelagica*
BREEDING BIRD. COMMON. Early date: Revere 4/11/72 (SF). Late date: 11/2/88 (FB, RB). High count 8,000+ Coopersburg 9/80 (TF). Found in cities, towns, and open areas.

Ruby-throated Hummingbird   *Archilochus colubris*
BREEDING BIRD. COMMON. Early date: Little Gap Bird Observatory 3/29/97 (BSi). Late date: 10/19/58 (CB). High count: 42-Bake Oven Knob 8/28/73 (RW). Prefers brushy fields and meadows.

Rufous Hummingbird   *Selasphorus rufus*
CASUAL. New to area. Four records: Allentown 8/14/95 (J&NB-photo), Trexlertown late Sept. 96 – 1/12/97 (RD, BLM, mobs-photo), Nazareth 11/14-12/7/00 (RW, photo, mobs), and Williams Twp. 11/9-17/01 (AK, mobs, photo). Sightings at hummingbird feeders.

Belted Kingfisher   *Ceryle alcyon*
RESIDENT. COMMON. Rare in winter. Found along streams, rivers, lakes, and ponds.

Red-headed Woodpecker   *Melanerpes erythrocephalus*
RESIDENT. RARE, LOCAL, and declining. Primarily found in open areas with scattered large trees.

Red-bellied Woodpecker   *Melanerpes carolinus*
RESIDENT. COMMON. Found along forest edges, woodlots, and yards with larger trees.

Yellow-bellied Sapsucker *Sphyrapicus varius*
WINTER VISITOR. UNCOMMON. Early date: 8/25/83 (BSi). Late date: Monocacy Nature Center 5/17/90 (JZ). Two summer records: Leaser Lake 7/1/89 (K & DG) and 8/10/93 (JG, DG). Found in deciduous and mixed forest.

Downy Woodpecker *Picoides pubescens*
RESIDENT. COMMON. Found in forests, woodlots, and suburban yards with trees.

Hairy Woodpecker *Picoides villosus*
RESIDENT. FAIRLY COMMON. Found in forests and woodlots.

Black-backed Woodpecker *Picoides arcticus*
ACCIDENTAL. Three records: Trexlertown Pines 12/62-4/15/63 (mobs), Kresgeville 2/8/64 (GHi), and Baer Rocks 9/30 & 10/2/84 (KK, DS).

Northern Flicker *Colaptes auratus*
RESIDENT. COMMON. Found in forests, woodlots, fields with scattered trees. Often seen feeding on the ground.

Pileated Woodpecker *Dryocopus pileatus*
RESIDENT. UNCOMMON. Found in extensive mature forest areas.

Olive-sided Flycatcher *Contopus cooperi*
MIGRANT. RARE. Spring: 4/15/77 (CRE) – Quakertown Swamp 6/22/78 (BSi, mobs). Fall: Unami Creek Valley 7/25/88 (JH) – 10/14/81 (BLM). Found along forest edges and swamps. Often perched on dead branches or tree-tops.

Eastern Wood-Pewee *Contopus virens*
BREEDING BIRD. COMMON. Early date: 4/13/81 (CRE). Late date: 10/14/80 (DG, JG). Prefers mature deciduous forests.

Yellow-bellied Flycatcher *Empidonax flaviventris*
MIGRANT. RARE. Spring: 5/12/83 (RW) – 6/22/78 (BSi). Fall: 8/17/85 (SF) – 10/10/56 (CB). Found along forest edges and swamps.

Acadian Flycatcher *Empidonax virescens*
BREEDING BIRD. UNCOMMON. Early date: 5/5/80 (WC). Late date: 10/3/84 (BLM). Found in moist deciduous forest with dense understory.

Alder Flycatcher *Empidonax alnorum*
MIGRANT, possible Breeding Bird. Rare. Early date: Ross Twp. 5/16/93 (RW). Late date: Jordan Creek Parkway 10/5/93 (PM). All but one summer record are from the Kittatinny Ridge and north. Prefers wet brushy areas, wooded swamps.

Willow Flycatcher *Empidonax traillii*
BREEDING BIRD. FAIRLY COMMON. Early date: Shimerville 5/12/94 (RW). Late date: Green Lane Reservoir 8/29/01 (KFC). Prefers brushy meadows, shrub swamps.

Least Flycatcher *Empidonax minimus*
BREEDING BIRD. UNCOMMON. Early date: Allentown 4/28/88 (BLM). Late date: 10/10/81 (BLM). Prefers second growth and mature forests. Breeds at Penn Forest Reservoir.

Hammond's Flycatcher *Empidonax hammondii*
ACCIDENTAL. Two records: Schnecksville 12/23/66 (DH-specimen) and Monocacy Nature Center 11/18-12/21/00 (LF, JZ, RW-photo, mobs).

Dusky Flycatcher *Empidonax oberholseri*
ACCIDENTAL. One record: Kutztown 12/25/69 (Nagey 1971).

Eastern Phoebe *Sayornis phoebe*
BREEDING BIRD. COMMON. Early date: Point Phillips 2/10/00 (RW). Late date: Martins Creek 12/31/00 (RW). During mild winters this species may be present into early winter. Found in woodland and farmland; often nests under bridges and overhangs of buildings.

Ash-throated Flycatcher *Myiarchus cinerascens*
ACCIDENTAL. New to area. One record: Williams Twp. 11/24-12/16/97 (AK, FH-photo, mobs).

Great Crested Flycatcher *Myiarchus crinitus*
BREEDING BIRD. COMMON. Early date: 4/14/80 (RB, DC). Late date: 10/8/78 (BLM). Found in deciduous forest.

Western Kingbird *Tyrannus verticalis*
CASUAL. Four records: Harmony Twp. 9/18-19/82 (GH-photo), Seemsville 9/14/90 (RW), Jordan Creek Parkway 5/30/91 (JG, DG), and Beltzville State Park 6/27/97 (JaSi, BSi-photo). Found in tree lines along fields and forest edges.

Eastern Kingbird *Tyrannus tyrannus*
BREEDING BIRD. COMMON. Early date: Forks 4/15/94 (RW). Late date: 10/3-14/66 (JS). One winter sighting: Hereford 12/15/01 (SH). Found in open fields and meadows with scattered large trees and shrubs.

Scissor-tailed Flycatcher *Tyrannus forficatus*
ACCIDENTAL. Two records: Lopatcong Twp. 8/23/67 (GeH) and Lynn Twp. 8/10-9/12/86 (KG, mobs, photo).

Loggerhead Shrike *Lanius ludovicianus*
ACCIDENTAL. Few, if any records in the past 15 years. Last reported sighting was at Leaser Lake 10/11/76 (RW). Any shrike observed April through October should be carefully studied and well documented. Found in open meadows with shrubs and bushes.

Northern Shrike *Lanius excubitor*
WINTER VISITOR. IRRUPTIVE. Early date: Green Lane Reservoir 11/1/99 (PS, CZ). Late date: Green Lane Reservoir 4/8/01 (KSt). Most recent irruptions during winters of 1995/1996 and 1999/2000. Found in open meadows with shrubs and bushes.

White-eyed Vireo *Vireo griseus*
BREEDING BIRD. UNCOMMON and declining. Early date: 4/21/87 (AK). Late date: 10/24/76 (RW). Found in moist second growth forest and shrubby areas.

Yellow-throated Vireo *Vireo flavifrons*
BREEDING BIRD. UNCOMMON. Early date: 4/26/80 (GLF). Late date: 10/12/80 (RG). Found in moist mature forest and riparian corridors.

Blue-headed Vireo *Vireo solitarius*
BREEDING BIRD. FAIRLY COMMON. Early date: Upper Perkiomen Valley Park 3/11/00 (P&AGu). Late date: 11/11/72 (RW). Breeds north of the Kittatinny Ridge in mixed forest.

Warbling Vireo   *Vireo gilvus*
BREEDING BIRD. FAIRLY COMMON. Early date: Monocacy Nature Center 4/22/01 (LF). Late date: Jordan Creek Parkway 10/5/93 (PM). Found in open areas with scattered trees, often along waterways.

Philadelphia Vireo   *Vireo philadelphicus*
MIGRANT. RARE. Spring: Bethlehem 4/19/89 (DG, JE) – Unami Creek Valley 5/25/91 (JH). Fall: Monocacy Nature Center 8/25/00 (LF) – 10/25/82 (LM). Found in second growth forest and woodlots.

Red-eyed Vireo   *Vireo olivaceus*
BREEDING BIRD. COMMON. Early date: 4/13/78 (SS). Late date: Revere 11/6/90 (SF). Found in deciduous forests and woodlots.

Blue Jay   *Cyanocitta cristata*
RESIDENT. COMMON. High count: 3,447-Little Gap Bird Observatory 10/5/01 (KMi). Possible in any habitat.

American Crow   *Corvus brachyrhynchos*
RESIDENT. COMMON. High count: 23,907-Bethlehem 12/26/81 (pers. comm. D&EM). Possible in any habitat.

Fish Crow   *Corvus ossifragus*
RESIDENT. FAIRLY COMMON. High count: 100+ Green Lane Reservoir 10/30/98 (KFC). This species has increased dramatically during the past 15 years. Possible in any habitat. Identified by call.

Common Raven   *Corvus corax*
RESIDENT. UNCOMMON. Only known nesting location is the Delaware Water Gap. High count: 13-Little Gap Bird Observatory 9/3/01 (AMi, KMi). Most seen along the Kittatinny Ridge during migration.

Horned Lark   *Eremophila alpestris*
RESIDENT. UNCOMMON. High count: 2,000-Alburtis 2/9/00 (A&JM). Most often seen in winter on bare fields, especially where manure has been spread. Local and more difficult to find in summer.

Purple Martin   *Progne subis*
BREEDING BIRD. UNCOMMON and local. Early date: 3/22/54 (CM). Late date: Green Lane Reservoir 9/26/90 (RW). Found in large, open fields, often near lakes and ponds.

Tree Swallow   *Tachycineta bicolor*
BREEDING BIRD. COMMON. Early date: 3/6/83 (KK, EW). Late date: Martins Creek 11/24/91 (FB, AK). High count: 3,000+ Henningsville 7/14/01 (PGS). Found in open areas, most often near water.

Violet-green Swallow   *Tachycineta thalassina*
ACCIDENTAL. New to area. One record: Penn Forest Reservoir 8/15/95 (JH).

Northern Rough-winged Swallow   *Stelgidopteryx serripennis*
BREEDING BIRD. FAIRLY COMMON. Early date: Chain Dam 3/25/00 (RW). Late date: Easton 11/11/01 (RW). Found along waterways, especially near bridge and road culverts.

Bank Swallow *Riparia riparia*
BREEDING BIRD. UNCOMMON. Early date: 3/28/80 (LM). Late date: 9/24/89 (GLF). High count: 1000+ Green Lane Reservoir 5/11/83 (GAF). 250 nesting burrows at Portland 5/16/93 (RW). Found along waterways with steep eroded banks, and over lakes and rivers during migration.

Cliff Swallow *Petrochelidon pyrrhonota*
BREEDING BIRD. UNCOMMON. Early date: Green Lane Reservoir 3/31/92 (DG, JG). Late date: Emmaus 10/16/92 (JH). High count: 66 active nests at Beltzville State Park June 1994 (BSi). Nests under bridges, generally over water.

Barn Swallow *Hirundo rustica*
BREEDING BIRD. COMMON. Early date: Nockamixon State Park 3/30/93 (SF). Late date: Nockamixon State Park 11/12/92 (SF). Found in large meadows and agricultural fields; nests under overhangs and in outbuildings.

Carolina Chickadee *Poecile carolinensis*
RESIDENT. COMMON. The breeding chickadee in the Unami Creek Valley and at Green Lane Reservoir. This species is expanding northward, and caution should be used when identifying chickadee species. Identification is especially problematic as hybridization between the two chickadee species is well documented and both species sing the other's song. Found in forests and woodlots.

Black-capped Chickadee *Poecile atricapillus*
RESIDENT. COMMON. This species replaces Carolina Chickadee in the northern portion of the area and on mountain ridges in the southern areas. Extends range farther south during winter months. Found in forests, woodlots, and suburban areas.

Boreal Chickadee *Poecile hudsonicus*
CASUAL. At least 12 records between 1975 and 1982; none since. Early date: Bake Oven Knob 10/21/75 (RW). Late date: Nockamixon State Park 4/13/78 (RF). High count: 4-Wild Creek Reservoir 12/29/81 (RW, BSi-calls recorded). Found in forests and woodlots.

Tufted Titmouse *Baeolophus bicolor*
RESIDENT. COMMON. Found in forests, woodlots, and suburban areas.

Red-breasted Nuthatch *Sitta canadensis*
RESIDENT. UNCOMMON. Rare local breeder in extensive coniferous forests. Most often seen fall through spring. More numerous in some years than others. High count: 25-Nockamixon State Park 10/18/88 (B&NM).

White-breasted Nuthatch *Sitta carolinensis*
RESIDENT. COMMON. Found in forests, woodlots, and suburban areas.

Brown Creeper *Certhia americana*
RESIDENT. UNCOMMON. Rare and local during breeding season. Found in forests and woodlots with mature trees.

Carolina Wren *Thryothorus ludovicianus*
RESIDENT. COMMON. Found in second growth forests, woodlots, and suburban areas.

Bewick's Wren *Thryomanes bewickii*
EXTIRPATED. Four sight records prior to 1958. Only recent report Jordan Creek Parkway 5/12/01 (AJ, JSo). This species' range has decreased over the past 50 years and any sightings need thorough documentation.

House Wren   *Troglodytes aedon*
BREEDING BIRD. COMMON. Early date: Neffs 3/13/89 (DSa). Late date: 10/21/79 (FB). A number of winter records. Found in second growth forests, woodlots, and suburban areas.

Winter Wren   *Troglodytes troglodytes*
RESIDENT. UNCOMMON WINTER VISITOR and Rare Breeding Bird. Reported to have nested in the Penn Forest Reservoir area in 1979 (RW), Walter Tract 1985 (FB), and Smith Gap in 1990, 1992 (RW). Very secretive; found in brush piles, stone walls, and thick tangles.

Sedge Wren   *Cistothorus platensis*
CASUAL. Four records: Alburtis 8/13/47 (CM, mobs), Quakertown Swamp 5/24/59 (CM, RM), Bear Swamp 5/8-9/94 (SLa, mobs), and one nesting record near Jacobsburg State Park 5/21-8/31/96 (RW-photo, mobs). Prefers wet grassy meadows.

Marsh Wren   *Cistothorus palustris*
MIGRANT. RARE. Formerly bred at Quakertown Swamp. Spring: Beltzville State Park 4/20/85 (SBo, RW) – Minsi Lake 6/20/84 (SBo). Fall: Nazareth 9/24/97 (RW) – Green Lane Reservoir 11/21/95 (KFC). Current nesting status unknown. Only two recent summer records: Green Lane Reservoir 8/1/83 (RW) and a singing bird in Heidelberg Twp. June 1996 (RW). Found in swamps and densely vegetated marshes.

Golden-crowned Kinglet   *Regulus satrapa*
RESIDENT. FAIRLY COMMON. Mostly found in migration, rare in summer. High count: 50-Jacobsburg State Park 4/12/83 (T&GM). Known breeding locations: Scott's Mt. and Wild Creek Reservoir. Prefers conifers.

Ruby-crowned Kinglet   *Regulus calendula*
MIGRANT, WINTER VISITOR. FAIRLY COMMON. Found mostly in migration. Early date: 9/2/75 (RW). Late date: 5/15/82 (T & BK). One summer record: Allentown 7/1/91 (J&NB). Found in deciduous and mixed forests and woodlots.

Blue-gray Gnatcatcher   *Polioptila caerulea*
BREEDING BIRD. COMMON. Early date: Jordan Creek Parkway 3/31/91 (AJ). Late date: Green Lane Reservoir 11/13/88 (GLF). One winter record: 12/16/78 (J&EP). Most common along forested river and creek valleys, especially along the Unami Creek Valley.

Eastern Bluebird   *Sialia sialis*
RESIDENT. FAIRLY COMMON. Increasing due to nest box trails. High count: 60-Green Lane Reservoir 12/82 (NT). Found in agricultural fields, forest edges, and open suburban areas.

Mountain Bluebird   *Sialia currucoides*
ACCIDENTAL. New to area. Two records: Beltzville State Park 12/16/84-3/22/85 (RW-photo, mobs) and Beltzville State Park 12/22/85-1/26/86 (RW, mobs).

Townsend's Solitaire   *Myadestes townsendi*
ACCIDENTAL. New to area. Two documented records: Little Gap 1/18/86 (JPu-photo) and Revere 3/22-23/93 (SF, GD-photo, mobs). Sightings of this species increasing in recent years throughout the northeast. Requires careful documentation.

Veery   *Catharus fuscescens*
BREEDING BIRD. FAIRLY COMMON. Early date: Revere 4/27/94 (SF). Late date: Fogelsville 10/21/90 (PE). One winter record: Bethlehem-Hellertown-Easton Christmas Bird Count 1971. Found in moist deciduous forest.

Gray-cheeked Thrush *Catharus minimus*
MIGRANT. RARE. Spring: Allentown 4/28/90 (BLM) – 6/3/84 (GAF). Fall: 9/13/83 (BLM) – 10/28/83 (BLM). Moist deciduous forest. Bicknell's Thrush *Catharus bicknelli*, was split from Gray-cheeked Thrush and though identification is problematic, this species should not be ruled out as a possible migrant through our area.

Swainson's Thrush *Catharus ustulatus*
MIGRANT. UNCOMMON. Spring: 4/13/58 (CM) – 6/3/79 (FB). Fall: 8/6/78 (FB) – 11/23/80 (BSi, CK, TK). One summer record: Wild Creek Reservoir 7/12/87 (BR). Two winter records: Lehigh Valley Christmas Bird Count 1974 and 2/9/91 (JH). Found in moist deciduous forest.

Hermit Thrush *Catharus guttatus*
RESIDENT. FAIRLY COMMON. Local breeder in the Penn Forest and Wild Creek Reservoir areas. Most abundant during migration and present during mild winters. Prefers moist deciduous and mixed forests. In winter also found in dense cover along field edges.

Wood Thrush *Hylocichla mustelinus*
BREEDING BIRD. COMMON. Early date: 4/16/80 (DC, RB). Late date: Unami Creek Valley (10/14/72 (GAF). One winter record: Bethlehem-Hellertown-Easton Christmas Bird Count 12/30/78. Found in moist deciduous forest.

American Robin *Turdus migratorius*
RESIDENT. COMMON. Possible in any habitat.

Varied Thrush *Ixoreus naevia*
ACCIDENTAL. Two records: Lower Saucon twp. 1/21-2/3/78 (B & JO-photo) and Nockamixon State Park 2/79 (GD).

Gray Catbird *Dumetella carolinensis*
BREEDING BIRD. COMMON. Early date: 4/13/85 (FB). Late date: unknown. Numerous winter records. Found in hedgerows, brushy areas, forest edges, and more vegetated suburban areas.

Northern Mockingbird *Mimus polyglottos*
RESIDENT. COMMON. Hedgerows, brushy areas, forest edges, and suburban areas.

Brown Thrasher *Toxostoma rufum*
BREEDING BIRD. UNCOMMON and local. Early date: Whitehall 3/27/71 (RW). Late date: Unknown. A few winter records. Found in brushy hedgerows and overgrown fields.

European Starling *Sturnus vulgaris*
RESIDENT. COMMON. Found in most habitats.

American Pipit *Anthus rubescens*
MIGRANT. UNCOMMON. Spring: Niantic 2/8/99 (KFC) - Green Pond 5/24/93 (RW). Fall: Green Lane Reservoir 9/3/01 (A&JM) – Martins Creek 12/31/00 (RW). High count: 500-Lower Nazareth Twp. 4/12/78 (BSi). One summer record: 6/3/53 (CM). Two winter records: Nazareth 1/6/95 (RW) and Martins Creek 1/6-21/01 (SBo, RW). Found in large open fields and mud flats.

Sprague's Pipit *Anthus spragueii*
ACCIDENTAL. One report: Green Lane Reservoir 4/20/63 (J&EP).

Cedar Waxwing *Bombycilla cedrorum*
RESIDENT. FAIRLY COMMON. High count: 1,000+Beltzville State Park 12/26/85 (SS). Usually found in flocks near cedars and fruit trees.

Blue-winged Warbler   *Vermivora pinus*
BREEDING BIRD. FAIRLY COMMON. Early date: Revere 4/23/77 (SF). Late date: 10/5/82 (SS). Found along brushy edges, overgrown fields, and power-line corridors.

Golden-winged Warbler   *Vermivora chrysoptera*
BREEDING BIRD. RARE. Breeds locally in the Penn Forest area. Early date: Jordan Springs 4/30/40 (CM). Late date: 10/4/83 (BLM). Prefers brushy edges, overgrown fields, and power-line corridors.

Tennessee Warbler   *Vermivora peregrina*
MIGRANT. UNCOMMON. Spring: 4/21/81 (T&BK) – 5/27/73 (RW). Fall: 7/23/77 (FB) – 10/22/79 (SS). Found in deciduous forests.

Orange-crowned Warbler   *Vermivora celata*
MIGRANT. RARE. Spring: 5/2/70 (GAF) – Emmaus 5/17/88 (JH). Fall: Fogelsville 8/25/92 (PE) – Green Lane Reservoir 11/6/99 (B&NM). Two winter records: Nockamixon State Park 12/4/91 (RFr, DMc) and Red Hill 1/25-3/2/00 (GLF, TMe). Found in brushy areas, overgrown fields, and forest edges.

Nashville Warbler   *Vermivora ruficapilla*
MIGRANT. UNCOMMON. Spring: Monocacy Nature Center 4/21/95 (LF, ST) – Unami Creek Valley 5/22/88 (GLF). Fall: 8/13/89 (BLM) – Allentown 11/12/93 (J&NB). Three summer records: (all from Penn Forest Reservoir) 6/26/73 (RW, WW), 6/14/81 (BSi), and 6/26/84 (SBo, BSi, RW). One winter record: Walter Tract 12/14-21/80 (FB, SS). Found in second growth forests.

Northern Parula   *Parula americana*
BREEDING BIRD. FAIRLY COMMON. Early date: Monocacy Nature Center 3/13/91 (LF). Late date: 10/17/92 (J&NB). Found in deciduous and mixed forests, often along waterways.

Yellow Warbler   *Dendroica petechia*
BREEDING BIRD. FAIRLY COMMON. Early date: 4/8/84 (SR). Late date: Jordan Creek Parkway 10/28/89 (PE, BLM). Found in moist brushy areas, often associated with willows.

Chestnut-sided Warbler   *Dendroica pensylvanica*
BREEDING BIRD. FAIRLY COMMON. Early date: Unami Creek Valley 4/28/94 (KFC). Late date: 11/19/79 (RW). Found in brushy areas, power-line corridors through deciduous forests.

Magnolia Warbler   *Dendroica magnolia*
BREEDING BIRD. FAIRLY COMMON. Only known breeding location is at Wild Creek Reservoir. Most abundant during migration. Early date: 4/28/89 (CRE). Late date: 10/18/80 (FB). Found in forests and woodlots.

Cape May Warbler   *Dendroica tigrina*
MIGRANT. UNCOMMON. Spring: 4/28/79 (SS) – 5/22/80 (FB). Fall: 8/12/78 (RW) – 10/22/83 (FB). One summer record: Wild Creek Reservoir 6/14/81 (BSi). Two winter records: Wescosville 12/20-21/83 (JAF), Nazareth 1/19-31/99 (NW, RW, DDe). Found in forests and woodlots, especially in spruce.

Black-throated Blue Warbler   *Dendroica caerulescens*
MIGRANT. FAIRLY COMMON. Spring: 4/19/82 (BK) – 5/28/79 (SS). Fall: Monocacy Nature Center 8/15/93 (LF, ST) – 10/20/81 (LM). One winter record: Cherryville 12/17/89 (SR). Two summer records, both from Penn Forest Reservoir 6/18/85 (RW) and 7/8/00 (RW). Found in forests and woodlots.

Yellow-rumped Warbler *Dendroica coronata*
WINTER VISITOR. COMMON. Most numerous during migration. Early date: Green Lane Reservoir 8/2/93 (GLF) Late date: 5/30/80 (MSt). Nested at Wild Creek Reservoir 1983, and at least four June records of singing birds (RW). High count: 1,000 Green Pond 5/2/80 (WC). Found in deciduous and mixed forest, Eastern Red-cedar stands.

Black-throated Green Warbler *Dendroica virens*
BREEDING BIRD. FAIRLY COMMON. Early date: 4/21/80 (DC, RB). Late date: 11/7/82 (DHe). Local breeder in northern portion of coverage area, migrant elsewhere. Found in deciduous and mixed forests.

Townsend's Warbler *Dendroica townsendi*
ACCIDENTAL. One record: Harmony Twp. 12/4-6/79 (GH-photo).

Blackburnian Warbler *Dendroica fusca*
BREEDING BIRD. UNCOMMON. Local breeder in the Penn Forest and Wild Creek Reservoir areas. Most abundant during migration. Early date: Coopersburg 4/27/89 (CM). Late date: 10/3/65 (DH). Found in deciduous and mixed forests.

Yellow-throated Warbler *Dendroica dominica*
BREEDING BIRD. RARE AND LOCAL. Early date: Bethlehem 4/7/00 (RW). Late date: 9/17/52 (CM). Local breeder along Delaware and Lehigh Rivers and in the Unami Creek Valley. Prefers mature riparian forests.

Pine Warbler *Dendroica pinus*
BREEDING BIRD. UNCOMMON. Early date: 3/14/79 (D&EM). Late date: 11/28/57 (CM). At least four winter records. Local breeder at Wild Creek, Penn Forest Reservoir, Unami Creek Valley, and Nockamixon State Park. Found in larger stands of conifers, as well as deciduous forests and woodlots during migration.

Prairie Warbler *Dendroica discolor*
BREEDING BIRD. FAIRLY COMMON. Early date: Monocacy Nature Center 4/10/94 (LF). Late date: 10/21/81 (KK). One winter record: Whitehall 12/4/84 (RW). Found in brushy areas, especially where Eastern Red-cedar stands are present.

Palm Warbler *Dendroica palmarum*
MIGRANT. FAIRLY COMMON. Spring: East Bangor Dam 3/24/90 (DDe) – Green Lane Reservoir 5/12/89 (KFC). Fall: 9/12/81 (WC) – 10/31/92 (TF). One summer record: Upper Perkiomen Valley Park 8/4/96 (RG). Three winter records: 12/6/84 (AK), Green Lane Reservoir 12/31/94 (LRh), and Williams Twp. 1/18/00 (AK). Found along edges of fields and woodlots; in undergrowth of forested areas.

Bay-breasted Warbler *Dendroica castanea*
MIGRANT. UNCOMMON. Spring: 4/28/90 (DDe) – 6/3/79 (FB). Fall: 8/16/77 (RW) – 10/22/83 (FB). Found in coniferous and mixed forest.

Blackpoll Warbler *Dendroica striata*
MIGRANT. FAIRLY COMMON. Spring: Monocacy Nature Center 4/24/96 (LF, ST) – Jacobsburg State Park 6/26/97 (RW). Fall: 8/15/79 (SS) – 11/6/77 (D&EM). Found in deciduous and mixed forest.

Cerulean Warbler *Dendroica cerulea*
BREEDING BIRD. UNCOMMON. Early date: Smith's Gap 4/25/94 (RW). Late date: 9/19/80 (LM). Local breeder along the Kittatinny Ridge and the Delaware River. Found in mature deciduous forest.

Black-and-white Warbler *Mniotilta varia*
BREEDING BIRD. FAIRLY COMMON. Early date: 3/9/87 (AK). Late date: Monocacy Nature Center 10/23/96 (LF). Two winter records: 12/21/74 (TMu) and 1977 Bethlehem-Hellertown-Easton Christmas Bird Count. Found in deciduous forests.

American Redstart *Setophaga ruticilla*
BREEDING BIRD. FAIRLY COMMON. Early date: Allentown 4/21/89 (CRE). Late date: 10/28/73 (RW). Two winter records: 1974 Allentown Christmas Bird Count (BT) and a female near Hellertown 12/29/01, on the Bethlehem-Hellertown-Easton Christmas Bird Count. Found in moist deciduous forest and woodlots.

Prothonotary Warbler *Protonotaria citrea*
SUMMER VISITOR. RARE. No confirmed breeding known. Early date: 4/20/75 (WW). Late date: 9/3/38 (CB). Prefers riparian corridors with mature trees.

Worm-eating Warbler *Helmitheros vermivorus*
BREEDING BIRD. UNCOMMON. Early date: 4/26/84 (T&GM). Late date: 9/24/85 (SR). Prefers deciduous forest with dense understory and shrub layer.

Swainson's Warbler *Limnothlypis swainsonii*
ACCIDENTAL. Three records: Kirkridge 6/4/78 (RW, WW), Baer Rocks 9/11/82 (KK, AG), and Wi-Hi-Tuk Park, Easton 6/25/00 (FB, mobs).

Ovenbird *Seiurus aurocapillus*
BREEDING BIRD. COMMON. Early date: Revere 4/22/76 (SF). Late date: 10/25/79 (D&EM). Two winter records: 1971 Bethlehem-Hellertown-Easton Christmas Bird Count and Henningsville 12/21/91-1/10/92 (PGS-photo). Found in mature deciduous forest.

Northern Waterthrush *Seiurus noveboracensis*
MIGRANT. UNCOMMON. Spring: 4/2/78 (BSi) - Unknown. Fall: Green Pond 7/31/01 (RW) - 10/6/74 (RW). One winter record: 1980 Bethlehem-Hellertown-Easton Christmas Bird Count. Deciduous forests along streams and rivers.

Louisiana Waterthrush *Seiurus motacilla*
BREEDING BIRD. FAIRLY COMMON. Early date: Unami Creek Valley 3/21/89 (GLF). Late date: 9/7/81 (LM). One winter record: Sandt's Eddy 2/20/95 (DMi). Found in deciduous forests along streams and rivers.

Kentucky Warbler *Oporornis formosus*
BREEDING BIRD. UNCOMMON. Rare away from breeding areas. Early date: Monocacy Nature Center 4/26/01 (LF). Late date: 10/15/82 (AR-specimen). Prefers moist deciduous forest with dense understory and shrub layer.

Connecticut Warbler *Oporornis agilis*
MIGRANT. RARE. Spring: 5/2/37 (CM) - 5/20/80 (MSt). Fall: 8/20/79 (MSt-specimen) – Henningsville 10/11/98 (PGS). Only four spring records. Found in brushy areas, overgrown fields, and forest edges.

Mourning Warbler *Oporornis philadelphia*
MIGRANT. RARE. Spring: 5/10/82 (T & BK) – Monocacy Nature Center 6/10/98 (LF, ST). Fall: Monocacy Nature Center 8/12/96 (LF) – 10/8/54 (CM). Found in brushy areas, overgrown fields, and forest edges.

Common Yellowthroat   *Geothlypis trichas*
BREEDING BIRD. COMMON. Early date: 4/14/84 (SR). Late date: Copella 12/27/90 (RW). At least eight winter records. Found in brushy fields, woodlots, often near water.

Hooded Warbler   *Wilsonia citrina*
BREEDING BIRD. FAIRLY COMMON. Rare away from breeding areas. Early date: 4/22/80 (mobs). Late date: 9/10/78 (FB). Prefers moist deciduous forest with dense understory and shrub layer.

Wilson's Warbler   *Wilsonia pusilla*
MIGRANT. UNCOMMON. Spring: 4/30/83 (FB) – 6/1/72 (RW). Fall: Monocacy Nature Center 8/17/96 (LF) – Monocacy Nature Center 10/18/99 (LF). Three winter records: Bethlehem 12/10/60 (WT), 11/16/81 (GLF), and Easton 11/2 – 12/7/00 (AHo, CMe). Found in moist second growth forests, brushy areas.

Canada Warbler   *Wilsonia canadensis*
BREEDING BIRD. UNCOMMON. Early date: 5/1/90 (BLM). Late date: Lehigh Furnace Gap 10/14/91 (CRE). Nests locally at Penn Forest Reservoir. Prefers deciduous forests with dense understory and shrub layer.

Yellow-breasted Chat   *Icteria virens*
BREEDING BIRD. RARE AND LOCAL. Early date: 5/1/76 (FB). Late date: Allentown 10/30/95 (J&NB). One winter record: 1/56 (CB, RMan). Found in brushy areas and power-line corridors.

Summer Tanager   *Piranga rubra*
CASUAL. Ten records. Early date: Allentown 5/6/56 (CM). Late date: Baer Rocks 9/23/79 (KK).

Scarlet Tanager   *Piranga olivacea*
BREEDING BIRD. COMMON. Early date: 4/23/85 (SF). Late date: 10/10/81 (SS). Found in mature deciduous forests.

Western Tanager   *Piranga ludoviciana*
ACCIDENTAL. New to area. Two records: A female at Nockamixon State Park (north shore) 12/20-29/97 (DF, RW-photo, mobs) and a male at Nockamixon State Park (south shore) 12/21/97 (DA, RR).

Green-tailed Towhee   *Pipilo chlorurus*
ACCIDENTAL. New to area. One record: 11/27/94-3/1/95 near Green Lane Reservoir (LRh, RW-photo, mobs).

Eastern Towhee   *Pipilo erythrophthalmus*
BREEDING BIRD. COMMON. A few over-winter in mild years. Found in brushy fields and woodlots.

American Tree Sparrow   *Spizella arborea*
WINTER VISITOR. FAIRLY COMMON. Early date: 10/11/79 (SS, BLM). Late date: Jacobsburg State Park 5/8/90 (DG, JG). Found in brushy areas, forest edges, and fallow fields.

Chipping Sparrow   *Spizella passerina*
BREEDING BIRD. COMMON. Early date: Edelmans 2/28/92 (KS). Late date: 11/17/99 (LF). A few may over-winter during mild winters. Found in grassy fields, woodlots, and suburban yards especially with evergreen trees.

Clay-colored Sparrow   *Spizella pallida*
MIGRANT, WINTER VISITOR. RARE. New to area. First documented (Late date): Trachsville 5/9/85 (RW-photo). Early date: Nazareth 10/6/00 (RW). Usually one or two reported sightings per year. Found in brushy areas, forest edges, and fallow fields.

Field Sparrow   *Spizella pusilla*
RESIDENT. FAIRLY COMMON. Found in overgrown fields and brushy areas.

Vesper Sparrow   *Pooecetes gramineus*
BREEDING BIRD. UNCOMMON. Early date: Martins Creek 3/26/98 (RW). Late date: Bethlehem-Hellertown-Easton Christmas Bird Count 12/30/78. Found in large agricultural and fallow fields.

Lark Sparrow   *Chondestes grammacus*
ACCIDENTAL. Three records: Palmer Twp. 12/4/75 & 12/19/77 (WC, PF), and Williams Twp. 11/30/92 (AK).

Savannah Sparrow   *Passerculus sandwichensis*
RESIDENT. FAIRLY COMMON. Rare and local in winter. High count: 200-Green Lane Reservoir 10/15/88 (GLF). Found in agricultural fields and meadows.

Grasshopper Sparrow   *Ammodramus savannarum*
BREEDING BIRD. UNCOMMON. Early date: 4/12/81 (BK). Late date: 11/30/80 (BK). High count: 25-Wild Creek Reservoir 7/10/85 (AH). Prefers meadows and hayfields.

Henslow's Sparrow   *Ammodramus henslowii*
CASUAL. Former breeder. Five records since the 60s: Green Lane Reservoir 4/11/80 (GLF, RB), Green Lane Reservoir 10/13/96 (GAF), Williams Twp. 10/16/96 (AK), Williams Twp. 9/23/01 (AK), and Green Lane Reservoir 10/10/01 (JH). Prefers meadows and grasslands.

Le Conte's Sparrow   *Ammodramus leconteii*
ACCIDENTAL. New to area. One record: Green Lane Reservoir 11/3/94 (JPu).

Seaside Sparrow   *Ammodramus maritimus*
ACCIDENTAL. One record: Monocacy Nature Center 4/28/82 (BSi, BK-photo, mobs). This is the first documented PA record for the century.

Fox Sparrow   *Passerella iliaca*
WINTER VISITOR. UNCOMMON. Most numerous November and March. Early date: 9/27/80 (BLM). Late date: Emmaus 5/13/89 (JH). High count: 13-Whitehall 3/27/71 (RW). Found along brushy edges of forests and woodlots; overgrown fields.

Song Sparrow   *Melospiza melodia*
RESIDENT. COMMON. Found in brushy areas, forest edges, and suburban yards.

Lincoln's Sparrow   *Melospiza lincolnii*
MIGRANT. UNCOMMON. Spring: 4/6/82 (GLF) – 6/1/85 (AK). Fall: 8/20/79 (D&EM) – Fogelsville 11/11/90 (PE). High count: 12-Nazareth 9/24/96 (RW). Prefers meadows, wet fields, and forest edges.

Swamp Sparrow   *Melospiza georgiana*
RESIDENT. UNCOMMON. Found in shrub swamps, marshes, and wet meadows.

White-throated Sparrow   *Zonotrichia albicollis*
WINTER VISITOR. COMMON. Early date: Unami Creek Valley 9/15/74 (GAF). Late date: Monocacy Nature Center 5/22/97 (LF). At least five June records. Found along brushy areas, forest edges, and suburban yards.

White-crowned Sparrow *Zonotrichia leucophrys*
WINTER VISITOR. UNCOMMON. Early date: Green Lane Reservoir 9/23/01 (KFC). Late date: Nockamixon State Park 6/10/01 (BE). High count: 40+Martins Creek 1/16/99 (RW). Found along brushy areas and forest edges.

Golden-crowned Sparrow *Zonotrichia atricapilla*
ACCIDENTAL. One record: Easton 6/4/52 (AC-banded and photo, mobs).

Dark-eyed Junco *Junco hyemalis*
WINTER VISITOR. COMMON. Early date: Revere 9/4/92 (SF). Late date: Schnecksville 5/29/88 (BLM). Three summer records: Allentown 6/13/68 (MC), Hellertown (Reservoir Park) 6/79 (MSt), and Little Gap 8/25/01 (BWe). Found in brushy areas, forest edges, and suburban yards.

Lapland Longspur *Calcarius lapponicus*
WINTER VISITOR. RARE. Early date: 11/8/80 (PK). Late date: Graver's Hill 4/24/01 (MSc). High count: 50-Palmer Twp. 2/8/81 (WC). Found in large, sparsely vegetated agricultural fields, especially where manure has been spread. Usually associated with Snow Buntings and Horned Larks.

Snow Bunting *Plectrophenax nivalis*
WINTER VISITOR. RARE AND IRRUPTIVE. When present, can occur in large numbers (100+). Early date: 10/17/70 (JS). Late date: Bethlehem 5/3/72 (AJo in Scott and Cutler 1972). High count: 410-Point Phillips 12/20/98 (RW). Found in large, sparsely vegetated agricultural fields, especially where manure has been spread.

Northern Cardinal *Cardinalis cardinalis*
RESIDENT. COMMON. Found in bushy areas, forest edges, and suburban yards.

Rose-breasted Grosbeak *Pheucticus ludovicianus*
BREEDING BIRD. FAIRLY COMMON. Early date: 4/18/85 (BSi). Late date: 11/25/83 (MAT). Three winter records: Palmer Twp. a male on 1/9/80 (WC), a male Bethlehem Twp. 12/25-26/83 (mobs), and a female 12/30/85 (DDe). Found in deciduous forest.

Blue Grosbeak *Guiraca caerulea*
BREEDING BIRD. RARE. Sightings increasing. Early date: Coopersburg 4/30/94 (TM). Late date: Williams Twp. 10/5/01 (AK). Prefers overgrown brushy fields.

Indigo Bunting *Passerina cyanea*
BREEDING BIRD. COMMON. Early date: Revere 4/19/96 (SF). Late date: 10/15/83 (BLM). Found in overgrown brushy fields, and power-line corridors.

Painted Bunting *Passerina ciris*
ACCIDENTAL. Two records: Bethlehem 12/12/66 – 3/20/67 (mobs, specimen) and Point Phillips 4/25-28/96 (DDe-photo).

Dickcissel *Spiza americana*
WINTER VISITOR. RARE. Early date: Williams Twp. 9/1-10/92 (AK, mobs). Late date: Leaser Lake 5/27/89 (SS, AK). Three summer records: Alpha 7/7-16/88 (JE, mobs), Lyons 6/18/00 (CRE), and a singing male Leaser Lake 7/9/00 (DWo). High count: 2-Trexlertown 12/16/95 (AJ, BLM). Found in fallow fields, meadows, and brushy edges.

Bobolink *Dolichonyx oryzivorus*
BREEDING BIRD. UNCOMMON. Early date: 4/15/82 (R&KWa). Late date: Green Lane Reservoir 10/14/90 (KFC, GAF). High count: 2,000-Green Lane Reservoir 9/2/82. Found in hayfields and meadows.

Red-winged Blackbird *Agelaius phoeniceus*
RESIDENT. COMMON. Rare in winter. High count: 20,000+ Bake Oven Knob 10/23/82 (GLF). Found in meadows, marshes, swamps, and agricultural fields.

Eastern Meadowlark *Sturnella magna*
RESIDENT. UNCOMMON. Rare to absent in winter. High count: 87-Bath 2/25/73 (RW). Found in fallow fields, meadows, and hayfields.

Yellow-headed Blackbird *Xanthocephalus xanthocephalus*
CASUAL. Nine records. First reported: Palmer Twp. 3/28/74 (WC). Early date: Green Lane Reservoir 9/1-14/77 (RB, GAF). Late date: Williams Twp. 4/20-27/89 (AK, mobs). Found in mixed blackbird flocks during migration and in winter.

Rusty Blackbird *Euphagus carolinus*
MIGRANT, WINTER VISITOR. UNCOMMON. Early date: Green Lane Reservoir 9/25/91 (RW). Late date: 5/29/34 (CM). High count: 300-South Whitehall Twp. 12/17/83 (BT). Prefers wooded swamps and marshes.

Brewer's Blackbird *Euphagus cyanocephalus*
CASUAL. First reported: Allentown 11/30/76 – 1/6/77 (MC). About 15 reported sightings since 1977. Following the example of McWilliams and Brauning (2000), sightings of this species must be treated with caution. One recent accepted record: 3 on 11/14/1990 (AK).

Common Grackle *Quiscalus quiscula*
RESIDENT. COMMON. Rare in winter. Found in fields, meadows, suburban yards, and deciduous forests during migration.

Brown-headed Cowbird *Molothrus ater*
RESIDENT. COMMON. Found in fields, forest edges, and suburban yards.

Orchard Oriole *Icterus spurius*
BREEDING BIRD. UNCOMMON. Early date: Monocacy Nature Center 4/25/99 (LF). Late date: 9/23/50 (CB). Prefers open wet areas with scattered mature trees.

Baltimore Oriole *Icterus galbula*
BREEDING BIRD. FAIRLY COMMON. Early date: Monocacy Nature Center 4/23/01 (LF). Late date: Monocacy Nature Center 9/21/96 (LF). Several winter records. Found in open areas with scattered mature trees and forest edges.

Pine Grosbeak *Pinicola enucleator*
WINTER VISITOR. IRRUPTIVE. Early date: 10/26/61 (DH). Late date: 3/28/82 (BSi, BT). High count: 120-Beltzville State Park 12/81-2/82 (BSi, RW). Last reported area sighting: 3/27/86 (SR). This is the least expected of the winter finches. Found in coniferous and mixed forests, hedgerows, and evergreen plantations.

Purple Finch *Carpodacus purpureus*
YEAR-ROUND VISITOR. UNCOMMON. Most records from migration and winter. Summer records from the Penn Forest and Wild Creek areas. High count: 120-Unami Creek Valley 3/30/80 (DC, RB). Found in forests, forest edges, and at feeders in wooded areas.

House Finch *Carpodacus mexicanus*
RESIDENT. COMMON. Introduced Western species which was uncommon before 1970 and is now our most abundant "red" finch. Found in cities, towns, suburbs, and rural areas.

Red Crossbill *Loxia curvirostra*
WINTER VISITOR. IRRUPTIVE. Early date: Mid-October 81 (KK). Late date: Emmaus 5/11-6/2/98 (BG). High count: 100-Wild Creek Reservoir 1/8/82 (PBS, FW). Found in coniferous forests and plantations.

White-winged Crossbill *Loxia leucoptera*
WINTER VISITOR. IRRUPTIVE. Early date: Bethlehem 10/19-22/89 (DGe). Late date: 4/27/90 (JH). High count: 25+Trexler Park 4/8/82 (TM). Found in coniferous forests and plantations.

Common Redpoll *Carduelis flammea*
WINTER VISITOR. IRRUPTIVE. Early date: 11/13/80 (D&EM). Late date: 4/16/82 (WC). High count: 120-Danielsville 3/7/87 (BSi). Found along forest edges and weedy areas, especially where birch and alder are present.

Hoary Redpoll *Carduelis hornemanni*
CASUAL. Five records: Phillipsburg 1/8-2/28/69 (TMu), Bath 2/26/72 (RW), Palmer Twp. 2/6/78 (WC, PF), Perkiomenville 1/30/94 (RG), and Henningsville 2/18/96 (PGS, JMu). Found along forest edges and weedy areas, especially where birch and alder are present.

Pine Siskin *Carduelis pinus*
WINTER VISITOR. IRRUPTIVE. Early date: Bake Oven Knob 9/20/83 (RW). Late date: 6/1/90 (J&NB). High count: 215-Bake Oven Knob 11/21/87 (GLF). Found in coniferous and mixed forests, weedy fields, and brushy edges.

American Goldfinch *Carduelis tristis*
RESIDENT. COMMON. Found in brushy areas, weedy fields, and forests edges.

Evening Grosbeak *Coccothraustes vespertinus*
WINTER VISITOR. IRRUPTIVE. Formerly more regular. Early date: 9/9/79 (JF). Late date: 5/27/72 (MM). High count: 200-Wild Creek Reservoir 1/3/81 (DVOC). Found in mixed forests, woodlots, and feeders.

House Sparrow *Passer domesticus*
RESIDENT. COMMON. Found in most habitats, especially near human dwellings.

PROVISIONAL SPECIES LIST

The following species have also been reported in the Lehigh Valley and vicinity. They are not included in the Annotated List because they were listed as hypothetical in the 1984 edition or the record was not accepted by or never submitted to the Pennsylvania Ornithological Records Committee. Future official acceptance of these records will result in these species being added to the main list.

Brown Pelican   *Pelecanus occidentalis*
One unconfirmed sighting on a pond near Wind Gap 7/23/84 (PG).

White Ibis   *Eudocimus albus*
Two reports: An immature bird carefully studied 7/24/77 Leaser Lake (RW) and an adult flying over Minsi Lake 3/30/86 (SBo).

Pink-footed Goose   *Anser brachyrhynchus*
One report: Green Lane Reservoir 12/31/98-1/10/99 (SRo, mobs).

Barnacle Goose   *Branta leucopsis*
First documented Lake Muhlenberg 3/3-8 1982 (DS, DK-photo, mobs). Early date: Green Lane Reservoir 11/23-31 1996 (GLF, JH). Late date: Green Pond 3/20/96 (DMi). High count: 4 Green Lane Reservoir 2/15/98 (GAF). This species is often kept in captivity and its status in Pennsylvania is under review.

Harlequin Duck   *Histrionicus histrionicus*
One report: One male on the Lehigh River near Freemansburg 12/29/01 (JL), on the Bethlehem-Hellertown-Easton Christmas Bird Count.

Black Rail   *Laterallus jamaicensis*
One report: Weissport 9/7/98.

Franklin's Gull   *Larus pipixcan*
One report: Beltzville State Park 12/17/00 (DHa-under review).

Black-headed Gull   *Larus ridibundus*
One report: Nockamixon State Park 1/4/97 (AL, SF).

Mew Gull   *Larus canus*
One report: Nockamixon State Park 3/27-28/96 (JH, SF).

Thayer's Gull   *Larus thayeri*
One report: Green Lane Reservoir 4/3/96 (JH, GLF).

Black-legged Kittiwake   *Rissa tridactyla*
One report: Green Lane Reservoir 11/4/91 (NT).

Gull-billed Tern   *Sterna nilotica*
One report: Green Lane Reservoir 10/03/64 (CM).

Roseate Tern   *Sterna dougallii*
Two reports: 5/17/59 at Green Lane Reservoir (ER in Poole 1964) and Green Lane Reservoir 5/23/01 (JH).

Sooty Tern *Sterna fuscata*
One report: A juvenile bird flying over Williams Twp. 1999 (AK).

Chuck-will's-widow *Caprimulgus carolinensis*
Two reports: District Twp. 5/26/00 (CRE) and Bethlehem 5/18/00 (JZ).

Bohemian Waxwing *Bombycilla garrulous*
One report: Revere 2/28 – 3/13/69 (SF).

Black-throated Gray Warbler *Dendroica nigrescens*
One report: A well-studied individual Fullerton 9/20/72 (RW). One of four reported in PA during the fall/winter 1972/73.

Kirtland's Warbler *Dendroica kirtlandii*
One report: Williams Twp. 8/26/00 (AK, under review).

Spotted Towhee *Pipilo maculates*
One report: May 1997 at Muhlenberg College, Allentown (GAW, TR).

Lark Bunting *Calamospiza melanocorys*
One report: Bethlehem 12/29/90.

Nelson's Sharp-tailed Sparrow *Ammodramus nelsoni*
11/10-13/96 (BH, RW-photo). Not accepted by PORC because evidence could not confirm difference from Salt-marsh Sharp-tailed Sparrow.

Harris's Sparrow *Zonotrichia querula*
One report: Two sightings at the same location, Moorestown 12/15/01 (DDe, under review), 12/17/01 (AK).

Black-headed Grosbeak *Pheucticus melanocephalus*
One report: Williams Twp. 5/29/99 (AK).

Boat-tailed Grackle *Quiscalus major*
One report: Williams Twp. 5/16/96 (AK).

Bullock's Oriole *Icterus bullockii*
Two reports: Williams Twp. 11/12-13/96 (AK) and a female at Martin's Creek 10/22/01 (MSc-photo, under review).

BAR GRAPHS

The bar graphs are a visual representation of the seasonal variation of the occurrence and abundance of each species. They have been drawn to represent the typical status of each species in a given season, in the appropriate habitat and under optimal conditions. They provide more detailed information about the likelihood of seeing a species at any given time than the abundance and occurrence categories and they complement the species text accounts. For example, the Black Duck is a Year-round Visitor that is most observable from October to March. By looking at the bar graph for this species, the reader can determine the likelihood of encountering this species in any given time period.

Different line types are used in the bar graphs to indicate the different abundance categories. The status categories are the same as those used in the species text accounts (Annotated Species List), with the addition of Irregular. The **Irregular** line is used to show historical occurrences of a species where records were insufficient to assign one of the other categories. For Northern Bobwhite, our only species listed as Extirpated, we placed "x's" throughout the year. An asterisk (*) indicates an early, late, or isolated sighting record.

Common   expected to be seen on most field trips

Fairly Common   expected to be seen on more than half of all field trips

Uncommon   expected to be seen on less than half of all field trips

Rare   expected to be seen infrequently, some years not at all

Irregular   historical occurrences

Irruptive   more common in some years than in others

	Jan	Feb	Mar	Apr	May	June	July	Aug	Sept	Oct	Nov	Dec
Red-throated Loon			*			*					*	*
Pacific Loon				**	*						*	
Common Loon			*									
Pied-billed Grebe												
Horned Grebe			*		*					*		*
Red-necked Grebe	*	*			*					*		*
Eared Grebe				*						*		
Double-crested Cormorant	**		*									* *
Great Cormorant					*						*	
Anhinga				*								
American Bittern			*		*						*	
Least Bittern				*							*	
Great Blue Heron												
Great Egret			*							*		
Snowy Egret			*							*		
Little Blue Heron				*						*		
Tricolored Heron							**	*				
Cattle Egret				*								*
Green Heron			*							*		* **
Black-crowned Night-Heron		**	*							*		
Yellow-crowned Night-Heron				*				*				
Glossy Ibis			*			*		*				
Black Vulture												
Turkey Vulture												
Greater White-fronted Goose			*							*		

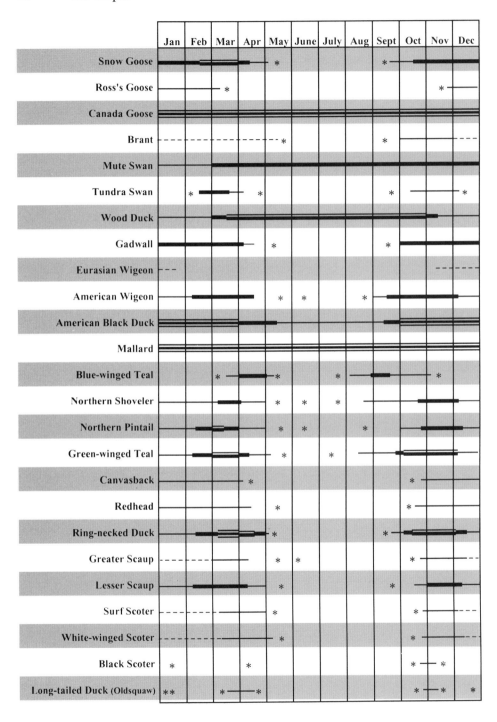

	Jan	Feb	Mar	Apr	May	June	July	Aug	Sept	Oct	Nov	Dec
Bufflehead					**	*		*		*		
Common Goldeneye					*					*		
Barrow's Goldeneye		*										
Hooded Merganser					*			*				
Common Merganser												
Red-breasted Merganser					*	*	* *		*			
Ruddy Duck		*			*				*			*
Osprey	*		*								*	
Swallow-tailed Kite					* *							
Mississippi Kite				****	* *							
Bald Eagle												
Northern Harrier					*		* *	*				
Sharp-shinned Hawk												
Cooper's Hawk												
Northern Goshawk												
Red-shouldered Hawk												
Broad-winged Hawk			*								*	
Swainson's Hawk									*		*	
Red-tailed Hawk												
Rough-legged Hawk				*						*		
Golden Eagle			*		*				*			
American Kestrel												
Merlin					*			*				
Gyrfalcon												
Peregrine Falcon			*		*			*			*	*

	Jan	Feb	Mar	Apr	May	June	July	Aug	Sept	Oct	Nov	Dec
Ring-necked Pheasant												
Ruffed Grouse												
Wild Turkey												
Northern Bobwhite	xxx	xxx	xxx	xxx	xxx	xxx	xxx	xxx	xxx	xxx	xxx	xxx
Yellow Rail					*					*		
King Rail					*							
Virginia Rail				*								*
Sora			*							*		
Purple Gallinule						* *						
Common Moorhen				*						*		*
American Coot												
Sandhill Crane					*		*			*		
Black-bellied Plover					*		*		*		*	
American Golden-Plover				*	*			*			*	
Semipalmated Plover					*		*		*		*	
Killdeer												
American Oystercatcher				*								
Black-necked Stilt					*							
American Avocet								*			*	
Greater Yellowlegs				*		*	*				*	
Lesser Yellowlegs				*			* *				*	
Solitary Sandpiper				*		*	*			*		
Willet					**		*	*	*			
Spotted Sandpiper				*						*		
Upland Sandpiper				*						*		

	Jan	Feb	Mar	Apr	May	June	July	Aug	Sept	Oct	Nov	Dec
Whimbrel				*				*	*			
Hudsonian Godwit								* — — — — —			*	
Ruddy Turnstone					*—*		* ————			*		
Red Knot					*—*			*—*				
Sanderling				*	—*		* ————				*	
Semipalmated Sandpiper					* ▭ *		* ▭————				*	
Western Sandpiper					*—*		*	▮			*	
Least Sandpiper				*	▭	* *		▭————			*	*
White-rumped Sandpiper					*— *		*	▮————			*	
Baird's Sandpiper							* ————	— — —		*		
Pectoral Sandpiper			*	▮ *			* ———	▮				*
Dunlin				*	▮ *			* ———		▮ *		
Stilt Sandpiper							* ———	▮			*	
Buff-breasted Sandpiper								* —→	*			
Ruff					*				*			
Short-billed Dowitcher				*	—*		*	▮		*		
Long-billed Dowitcher							* — — — —	— — —		*		
Common Snipe	————			▮	*	*	*	* ———				
American Woodcock		*	▮ ———							▮		*
Wilson's Phalarope					* — *		* ———	*				
Red-necked Phalarope					*—*			* ———		*		
Red Phalarope								*	*		*	
Laughing Gull				* ———							*	
Little Gull				* * *								
Bonaparte's Gull	————		▮	*		*		* *	*			

	Jan	Feb	Mar	Apr	May	June	July	Aug	Sept	Oct	Nov	Dec
Ring-billed Gull												
Herring Gull					*		* **	*				
Iceland Gull	*			*								
Lesser Black-backed Gull					*				*			
Glaucous Gull	***	**	*									*
Great Black-backed Gull					*	*	*	*	*			
Sabine's Gull										*		
Caspian Tern				*	*		*			*		
Common Tern				*	*	*	*	*			*	
Arctic Tern				*								
Forster's Tern				*		*	* *			*		
Least Tern						*	**	*				
Black Tern					*	*		*		*		
Dovekie		*									*	
Rock Dove												
Mourning Dove												
Black-billed Cuckoo					*					*		
Yellow-billed Cuckoo					*					*		
Barn Owl												
Eastern Screech-Owl												
Great Horned Owl												
Snowy Owl				*						*		
Barred Owl												
Great Gray Owl		*										
Long-eared Owl				*							*	

	Jan	Feb	Mar	Apr	May	June	July	Aug	Sept	Oct	Nov	Dec
Short-eared Owl				*						*		
Northern Saw-whet Owl												
Common Nighthawk		*									*	
Whip-poor-will				*							*	
Chimney Swift				*							*	
Ruby-throated Hummingbird			*							*		
Rufous Hummingbird								*	*		* *	
Belted Kingfisher												
Red-headed Woodpecker												
Red-bellied Woodpecker												
Yellow-bellied Sapsucker					*		*	* *				
Downy Woodpecker												
Hairy Woodpecker												
Black-backed Woodpecker		*							*			*
Northern Flicker												
Pileated Woodpecker												
Olive-sided Flycatcher				*		*	*			*		
Eastern Wood-Pewee				*						*		
Yellow-bellied Flycatcher					*	*		*		*		
Acadian Flycatcher					*					*		
Alder Flycatcher					*					*		
Willow Flycatcher					*			*				
Least Flycatcher					*					*		
Hammond's Flycatcher											*	*
Dusky Flycatcher												*

	Jan	Feb	Mar	Apr	May	June	July	Aug	Sept	Oct	Nov	Dec
Eastern Phoebe												
Ash-throated Flycatcher												
Great Crested Flycatcher												
Western Kingbird												
Eastern Kingbird												
Scissor-tailed Flycatcher												
Loggerhead Shrike												
Northern Shrike												
White-eyed Vireo												
Yellow-throated Vireo												
Blue-headed Vireo												
Warbling Vireo												
Philadelphia Vireo												
Red-eyed Vireo												
Blue Jay												
American Crow												
Fish Crow												
Common Raven												
Horned Lark												
Purple Martin												
Tree Swallow												
Violet-green Swallow												
Northern Rough-winged Swallow												
Bank Swallow												
Cliff Swallow												

	Jan	Feb	Mar	Apr	May	June	July	Aug	Sept	Oct	Nov	Dec
Barn Swallow			*								*	
Carolina Chickadee												
Black-capped Chickadee												
Boreal Chickadee				*						*		
Tufted Titmouse												
Red-breasted Nuthatch												
White-breasted Nuthatch												
Brown Creeper												
Carolina Wren												
Bewick's Wren					*							
House Wren				*						*		
Winter Wren												
Sedge Wren					* **				*			
Marsh Wren				*		*	*	*		*		
Golden-crowned Kinglet												
Ruby-crowned Kinglet					*		*		*			
Blue-gray Gnatcatcher				*							*	*
Eastern Bluebird												
Mountain Bluebird											* *	
Townsend's Solitaire	*		*									
Veery					*					*		*
Gray-cheeked Thrush				*		*		*		*		
Swainson's Thrush		*		*		*	*	*			*	*
Hermit Thrush												
Wood Thrush				*						*		*

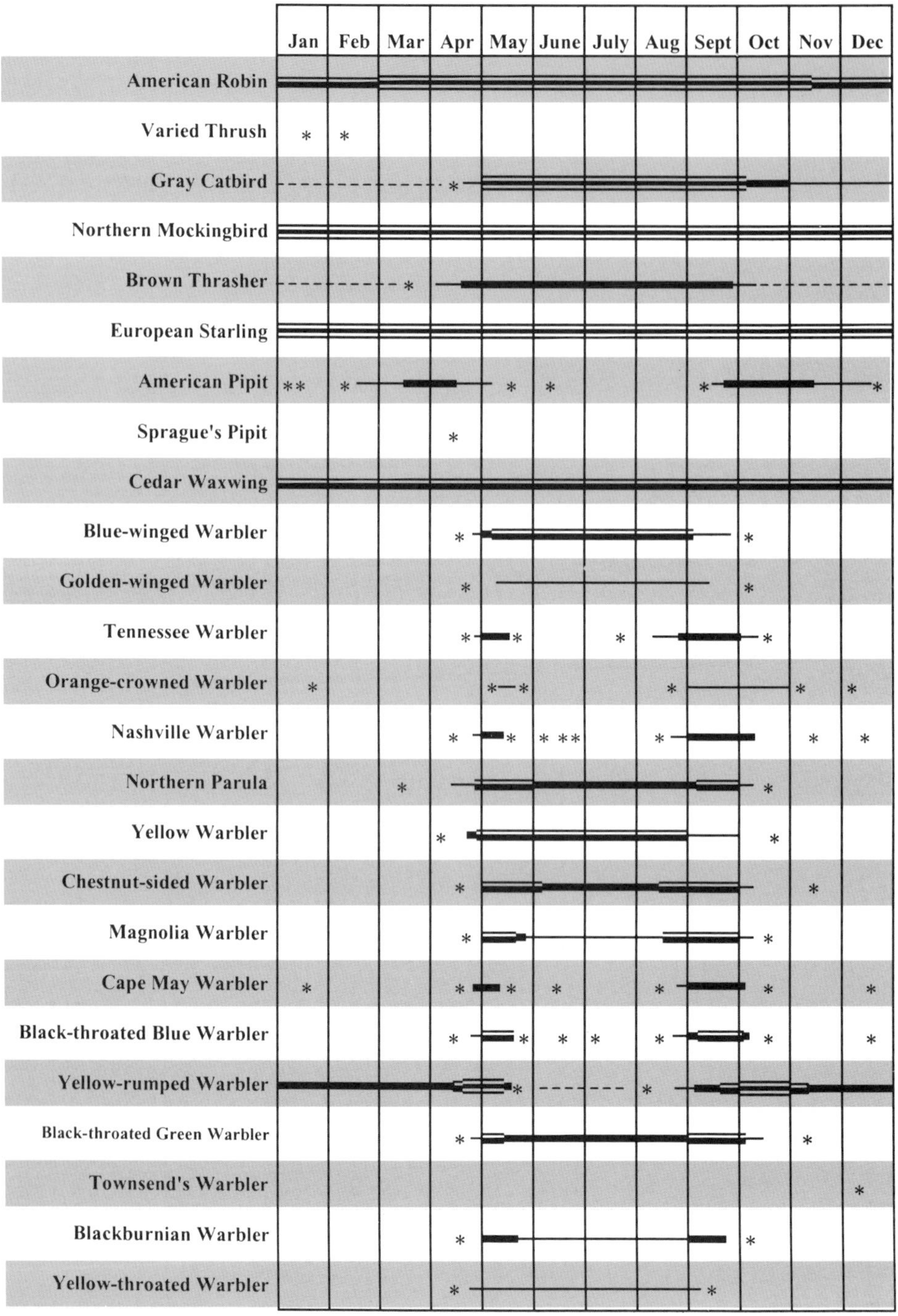

	Jan	Feb	Mar	Apr	May	June	July	Aug	Sept	Oct	Nov	Dec

American Robin

Varied Thrush

Gray Catbird

Northern Mockingbird

Brown Thrasher

European Starling

American Pipit

Sprague's Pipit

Cedar Waxwing

Blue-winged Warbler

Golden-winged Warbler

Tennessee Warbler

Orange-crowned Warbler

Nashville Warbler

Northern Parula

Yellow Warbler

Chestnut-sided Warbler

Magnolia Warbler

Cape May Warbler

Black-throated Blue Warbler

Yellow-rumped Warbler

Black-throated Green Warbler

Townsend's Warbler

Blackburnian Warbler

Yellow-throated Warbler

	Jan	Feb	Mar	Apr	May	June	July	Aug	Sept	Oct	Nov	Dec
Pine Warbler												
Prairie Warbler												
Palm Warbler												
Bay-breasted Warbler												
Blackpoll Warbler												
Cerulean Warbler												
Black-and-white Warbler												
American Redstart												
Prothonotary Warbler												
Worm-eating Warbler												
Swainson's Warbler												
Ovenbird												
Northern Waterthrush												
Louisiana Waterthrush												
Kentucky Warbler												
Connecticut Warbler												
Mourning Warbler												
Common Yellowthroat												
Hooded Warbler												
Wilson's Warbler												
Canada Warbler												
Yellow-breasted Chat												
Summer Tanager												
Scarlet Tanager												
Western Tanager												

	Jan	Feb	Mar	Apr	May	June	July	Aug	Sept	Oct	Nov	Dec
Green-tailed Towhee											*	
Eastern Towhee												
American Tree Sparrow					*					*		
Chipping Sparrow		*									*	
Clay-colored Sparrow					*					*		
Field Sparrow												
Vesper Sparrow				*								*
Lark Sparrow											*	* *
Savannah Sparrow												
Grasshopper Sparrow				*							*	
Henslow's Sparrow				*					*	***		
Le Conte's Sparrow										*		
Seaside Sparrow				*								
Fox Sparrow					*					*		
Song Sparrow												
Lincoln's Sparrow				*		*		*			*	
Swamp Sparrow												
White-throated Sparrow					*				*			
White-crowned Sparrow						*			*			
Golden-crowned Sparrow					*							
Dark-eyed Junco					*	**		*	*			
Lapland Longspur				*							*	
Snow Bunting					*					*		
Northern Cardinal												
Rose-breasted Grosbeak	*				*						*	* *

	Jan	Feb	Mar	Apr	May	June	July	Aug	Sept	Oct	Nov	Dec
Blue Grosbeak				*						*		
Indigo Bunting				*						*		
Painted Bunting				*								*
Dickcissel					*	*	**		*			
Bobolink				*						*		
Red-winged Blackbird												
Eastern Meadowlark												
Yellow-headed Blackbird				*					*			
Rusty Blackbird						*			*			
Brewer's Blackbird											*	
Common Grackle												
Brown-headed Cowbird												
Orchard Oriole				*					*			
Baltimore Oriole				*					*			
Pine Grosbeak				*						*		
Purple Finch												
House Finch												
Red Crossbill						*				*		
White-winged Crossbill				*						*		
Common Redpoll				*							*	
Hoary Redpoll	* **	*										
Pine Siskin						*			*			
American Goldfinch												
Evening Grosbeak					*				*			
House Sparrow												

68

COVERAGE AREA

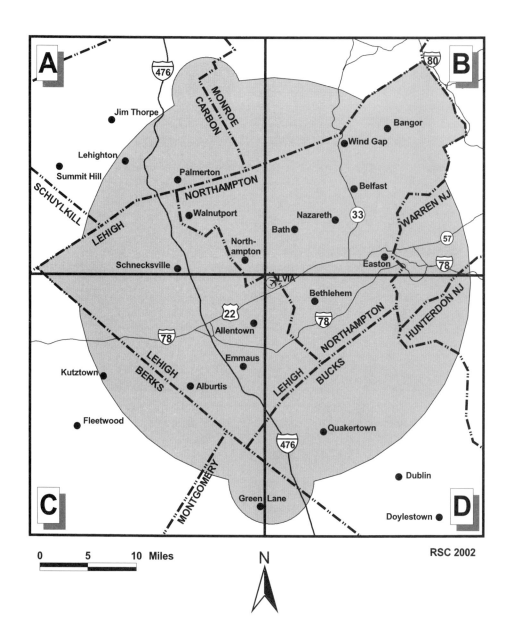

0   5   10 Miles

N

RSC 2002

SITE GUIDE LIST

QUAD A

1) Beltzville State Park
2) Wild Creek and Penn Forest Reservoirs
3) Little Gap
4) Lehigh River
5) Walnutport Area
6) Lehigh Furnace Gap
7) Bake Oven Knob
8) Bear (Baer) Rocks
9) Leaser Lake Recreational Area

QUAD B

10) Mount Bethel Fens
11) Minsi Lake Recreational Area, Bear Swamp Recreational Area, and East Bangor Dam
12) Cherry Valley-Portland-Mount Bethel Area
13) Smith Gap and Vicinity
14) Graver's Hill
15) Jacobsburg State Park
16) Albert Road Ponds
17) Martins Creek Environmental Preserve
18) Delaware River
19) Merrill Creek Reservoir and Environmental Preserve
20) Hugh Moore Park
21) Riverview Park
22) Green Pond

QUAD C

23) State Game Lands #205
24) Whitehall Parkway and Ironton Rail Trail/D & L Trail
25) Jordan Creek Parkway
26) Fogelsville Quarry and Dam
27) Trexler Park
28) Cedar Creek Park and Lake Muhlenberg
29) Little Lehigh Park (Lehigh Parkway)
30) Bob Rodale Cycling and Fitness Park
31) Rodale Experimental Farm
32) Smith Lane and Dorney Landfill
33) Kalmbach Memorial Park
34) Pool Wildlife Sanctuary
35) Reimert Memorial Bird Haven
36) Green Lane Park and Upper Perkiomen Valley Park

QUAD D

37) Oberly Road (Alpha, New Jersey)
38) Wy-Hit-Tuk Park
39) Monocacy Nature Center
40) Nisky Hill Cemetery
41) Sand Island
42) Lehigh Mountain Uplands
43) South Mountain Park
44) South Mountain Preserve (The Walter Tract)
45) Reservoir Park, Hellertown
46) Lake Warren
47) Lake Towhee County Park
48) Nockamixon State Park
49) Quakertown Swamp
50) Unami Creek Valley

QUAD A

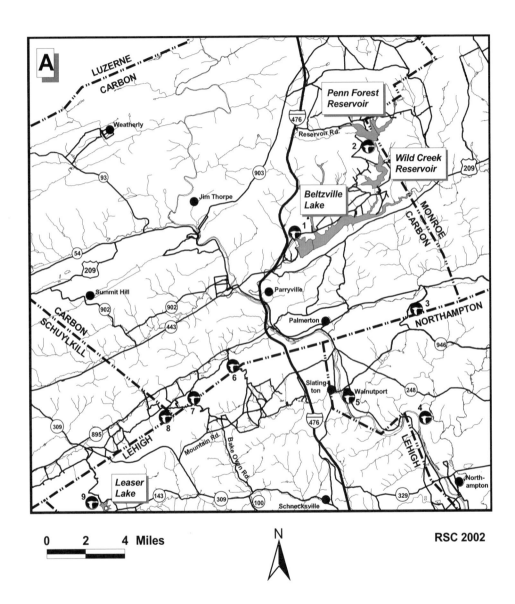

0 2 4 Miles

N

RSC 2002

QUAD B

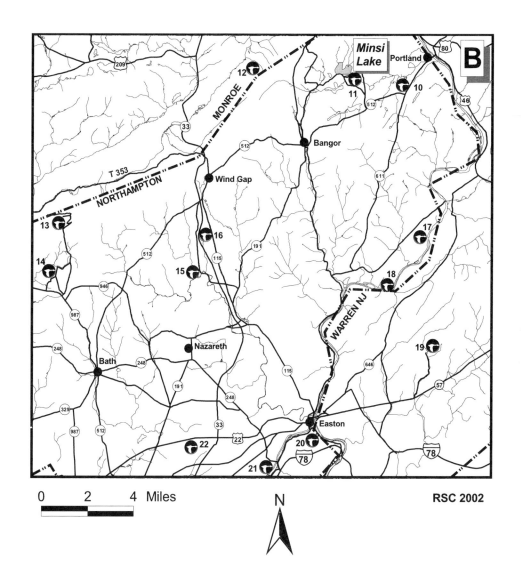

0   2   4 Miles

N

RSC 2002

QUAD C

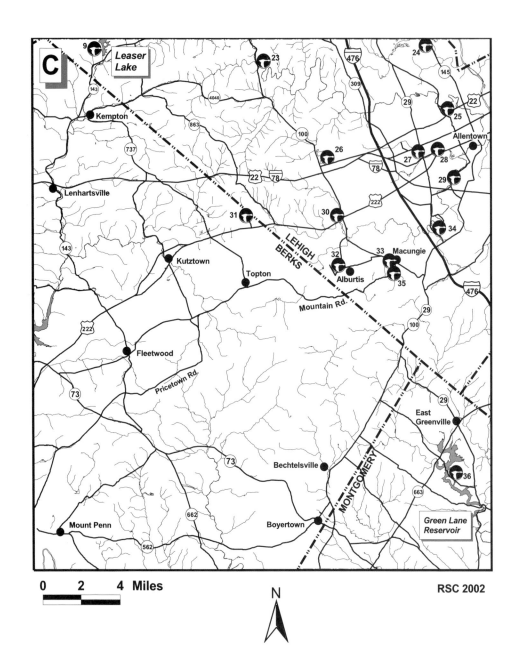

C

Leaser Lake

9

23

24

145

476

309

29

22

Kempton

4040

863

25

100

737

26

Allentown

27

28

22

78

78

Lenhartsville

222

29

143

31

30

34

LEHIGH

BERKS

32

33

Macungie

Kutztown

Alburtis

35

Topton

476

Mountain Rd.

29

222

100

Fleetwood

Pricetown Rd.

73

29

East Greenville

73

Bechtelsville

MONTGOMERY

36

663

662

Green Lane Reservoir

Mount Penn

Boyertown

562

0   2   4 **Miles**

N

RSC 2002

QUAD D

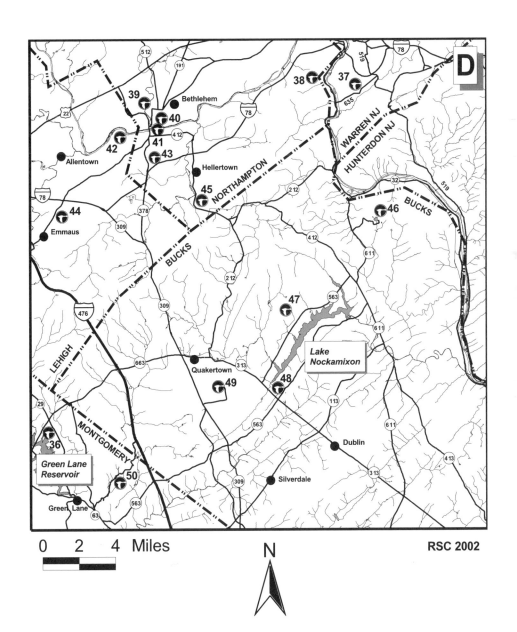

0   2   4   Miles

N

RSC 2002

SITE GUIDE INDEX

1. Beltzville State Park

Description. Beltzville is a 2,972-acre park with 949 acres of water, 19.8 miles of shoreline, and over 15 miles of trails. The southern side of the lakeshore is primarily steeply sloped with hemlock, white pine and rhododendron. Two access areas on this side have parking and trails that border the shoreline. There are also open brushy and secondary growth areas, as well as a few cultivated spots. The best birding, though, lies along the northern side of the lake. Cultivated fields, wildlife management food plots, deciduous and coniferous woodlots, old orchards, a swimming beach, waterfalls, small cattail areas, and creeks provide a diversified area easily accessible for birding.

Birds. The following provides a tour beginning at the western end of the lake, proceeding eastward along the northern border, and then covering the eastern end and southern border. To reach the starting point of the tour, see **Directions**. First-time visitors may prefer to skip the westernmost stop and go directly to the main park entrance (the second stop), where maps and other information may be obtained.

At the western end of the park below the dam breast are the two loops of the Sawmill Trail. To access the Lower (Blue) Loop, from the intersection of Pohopoco Dr. and Old Mill Rd., go 0.4 mi. on Old Mill Rd. and turn left into the first parking lot. Sawmill Creek meanders through the mixed mature forest here that is home to many woodland birds including Eastern Screech-Owl, Veery, Black-and-white Warbler, and other common birds. This area is protected from wind and is a good area to bird in spring migration when the winds in more exposed areas are strong. The Upper (White) Loop connects with the Lower Loop and is similar except that it crosses a field that is mowed irregularly. At the second parking lot, at the dead end of Old Mill Rd., a fisherman's path follows the stream and can be very productive in migration.

Returning to the intersection of Old Mill Rd. with Pohopoco Dr., turn right onto Pohopoco Dr. and continue 2.3 mi. to the main park entrance (pass the entrance to the U.S. Army Corps of Engineers facility). If you arrive early in the morning (before 7:30) and the gate is closed, you can park along the road and walk in. This road passes a deciduous forest on the right followed by mixed plantings which can be alive with warblers, flycatchers, and other migrants in spring when the morning sun warms the boughs. Pileated Woodpeckers have nested here, and Yellow-bellied Flycatchers have been seen more than once during migration, along with more than 10 warbler species at a time. Continue straight ahead to the parking lot and proceed to the grassy hillside behind the beach. Orchard Oriole has nested next to the parking lot. This beach area is usually only good after or during a storm. Shorebirds, gulls, and terns are possible here. Sanderlings, Red Knots, Laughing Gulls, and Common, Forster's, and Arctic Terns have been seen here along with other uncommon waterbirds. There is one record of American Oystercatcher. The open-water foragers can also be seen over the lake feeding or resting on the buoys.

The Environmental Interpretive Center, near the main park entrance (follow signs), has a year-round feeding station in the rear. There are paths around wild food plantings here, and many birds visit in winter. West of the beach in this vicinity is a cove that can harbor ducks,

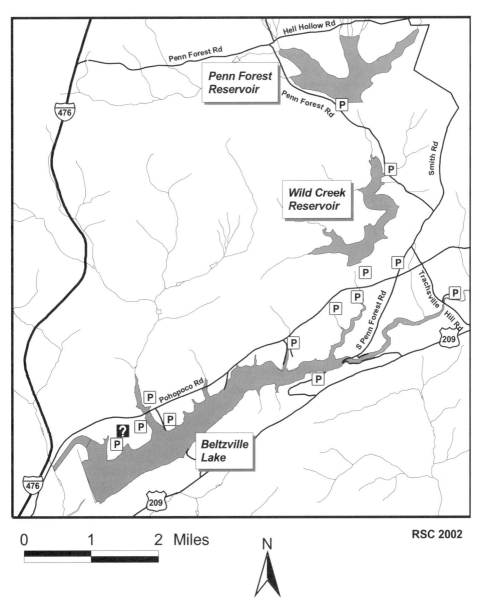

0   1   2   Miles   N

RSC 2002

grebes and other waterfowl, especially in winter when it is windy or when the ice has not completely covered the lake. Walk west along the shore towards the breast of the dam, scanning the water for waterbirds. At the westernmost tip of land, scan the cove to the right and the right-hand side of the dam breast. This is a regular resting area for waterfowl. Red-throated Loons, Great Cormorants, and Tundra Swans, as well as most of the dabbling and diving ducks, have been seen in this area.

At 0.3 mi. east of the park entrance on Pohopoco Dr., you will cross a bridge that houses a Cliff Swallow colony in nesting season. Turn left at Deer Ln. and take an immediate left into the dirt parking lot. In summer, walk down towards the water and south under the bridge to observe the swallows flying about and at their nests on the steel girders. Returning to Deer Ln., cross Pohopoco Dr. and go to the parking area a short distance farther at the lakefront. There is a small cattail patch east of the boat launch that has had American Bittern and Marsh Wren in migration, and occasional shorebirds when the water is low. A wide trail borders the lake to the east and wanders through shrubby habitat. Some years, Cedar Waxwings have nested in the oaks by the restrooms at the north end of the parking lot.

Traveling farther east along Pohopoco Dr., there are various parking areas in the PA Game Commission's Wildlife Management Area over the next two miles. These are excellent birding areas that have been planted with corn, safflower, Russian olive, pine, spruce, and other food-bearing crops. Sandhill Crane, Willow and Alder Flycatchers, Western Kingbird, Northern Shrikes, Mountain Bluebird, Redpolls, Pine Siskins, Pine and Evening Grosbeaks, and other uncommon birds have been seen in this large area. Rugged footwear and heavier clothes are advised for this area, as developed trails are few.

Almost at the eastern end of the lake, a total of 3.4 mi. from the main park entrance, there is a grassy parking area on the right providing access to the Christman Trail. This trail leads to a series of loop trails that are best traveled the first time with a copy of the trail guide available at the park headquarters. At the beginning of this trail is an old homestead spring that is open in the winter and overflows to an overgrown little valley that melds into forest for the remainder of the trails. Common woodland birds are regular here, and water bird activity generally increases during migration. You can reach the Wildcreek Trail from the Christman Trail and then head toward Wildcreek Falls. This is an exceptionally beautiful area that is picturesque and cool in the warm months. Keep a close eye on the footing because the rocks can be wet and slippery. The falls can also be reached from Wildcreek Trail parking lot 0.4 mi. further east on Pohopoco Dr.

Continuing 0.6 mi. on Pohopoco Dr. east from the Wildcreek parking area, you will come to Penn Forest Rd. Turn right on this road and stop along any of the grassy parking areas over the next 1.2 mi. You must bushwhack this area from the parking areas because trails are unmarked. The area is overgrown field bordering primary forest and can be thick, but it provides good edge birding. At the dead end, you can park and walk to the water where the lake narrows considerably. Woodland birds can be seen and heard well here because it is far from road traffic.

Returning to the intersection of Penn Forest Rd. with Pohopoco Dr., continue east on Pohopoco Dr. 0.4 mi. to Trachsville Hill Rd. Turn right and follow the road for 0.7 mi. to a parking lot on the left. From this parking lot, you can cross the road and enter coniferous forest bordering the southern edge of the lake via the Preacher's Camp Trail. The trailhead sign is not easily seen, but the trail goes close to the shore and is well marked with blazes after the first 30 yards. Broad-winged Hawks have nested here for many years, and many woodland species can be seen or heard heading toward the boat launch.

Continue 0.5 mi. farther south on Trachsville Hill Rd. and turn right (west) onto Interchange Rd. To access the Preacher's Camp boat launch area, take Interchange Rd./Rt. 209 south 2.5 mi. west and turn right at the gas station onto Preacher's Camp Rd. From the boat launch area you can travel west onto the Trinity Gorge Trail that crosses field, powerlines, small streams, and mixed and coniferous forest. A variety of birds can be found on this trail.

Directions. From the intersection of Rt. 22 with Rt. 476 (the Northeast Extension of the PA Turnpike), take Rt. 476 north 18.8 mi. to exit 34. Following the Beltzville State Park signs, turn left off the exit onto Rt. 209 North. Almost immediately, turn left at the park sign onto Harrity Rd. Go 0.1 mi. on Harrity Rd. and turn right onto Pohopoco Dr. To reach the first stop on the tour, follow Pohopoco Dr. 0.8 mi. and bear right onto Old Mill Rd.

To go directly to the main park entrance instead of the first tour stop, do not bear right onto Old Mill; continue on Pohopoco Dr. 2.3 mi. past this intersection and turn right into the park.

Notes. (1) The park office is 0.1 mi. on the west side of the park entrance (the first road to the right after the entrance). The recreational and trail guides available here will aid in finding parking areas and places where hunting is allowed. At the Environmental Interpretive Center/Visitor's Center (the second road to the right from the park entrance), maps of the park are in the front, and restrooms are on the east side. **(2)** This area can become very crowded in summer and is best avoided around the beach area except after a storm. There is almost always someone on the water with a boat, and you may need to scan the water from many spots to see where waterfowl are located. Winter and spring are probably the best times to bird here as the food is abundant and the people are few. **(3)** When birding the food plots on the Game Commission property, use caution during hunting season. The plots are arranged in rows, and someone shooting into one could easily penetrate the other side. **(4)** A scope is recommended unless you are only looking for land birds. **(5)** About two-thirds of the park is open to hunting in season; watch for signs.

2. Wild Creek and Penn Forest Reservoirs

Description. These two watershed reservoirs hold over 10 billion gallons of water and are administered by the Bethlehem Water Authority. More than 22 square miles of land are open to the public. (The lakes themselves -- Wild Creek with 304 acres of water and Penn Forest with 480 acres – are not public.) This area is remote and there are no human residents behind the Wild Creek Dam breast to the feeder streams of Penn Forest. Trails are abundant. Overlooks at both sites are opened by water company personnel daily from 8:00 a.m. to 3:00 p.m.

These locations can easily be visited in conjunction with a visit to Beltzville State Park. See the separate site description for the park.

Birds. The following provides a tour beginning at Wild Creek Reservoir and working from south to north. To reach the starting point of the tour, see **Directions.**

Follow the entrance road into Wild Creek Reservoir. At the end of the road you can see the reservoir. Bald Eagles have been spotted here many summers and during migration and in the winter. Diving ducks are regular in winter and migration. In summer, Pine and Prairie Warblers nest in this vicinity along with Hermit Thrush and Veery. These, along with other common nesting birds, can be found by walking the trails around the lakes.

Returning to Pohopoco Dr., continue 0.4 mi. east to its intersection with Penn Forest Dr. Turn left onto Penn Forest Dr. Follow this road about 2.0 mi. to the Rear Cove area. The Rear Cove, viewed from the road, is one of the better places to see waterfowl. Entrance to many of the roads in this area is barred with bright orange gates to keep the roads closed to vehicular traffic. Park to the side of any of these gates and walk in along the road. Plantings of pine and spruce are on both sides of the roads. Winter finches including crossbills, Evening Grosbeaks, and Common Redpolls can sometimes be found in the fall and winter. Pileated Woodpeckers and Golden-crowned Kinglets are year-round residents. Spring can give good views of Bay-breasted, Cape May, Magnolia, and other warblers in the spruce groves. Common Loons can be heard in spring as they rest on the water during migration. Common Mergansers nest here and Great Blue Herons can be seen throughout the year.

Continuing north on Penn Forest Dr., Gate 2 at Penn Forest is 1.3 mi. from the Rear Cove area. This area overlooks the reservoir. At night in the summer Barred and Great Horned Owls, Eastern Screech-Owls, and Whip-poor-wills can be heard. Be careful driving as Whip-poor-wills sit along the road. Coyotes have also been heard howling, and deer, turkey and Ruffed Grouse cross the road.

One of the more remote roads in the area can be reached by continuing on Penn Forest Dr. northwest from the Penn Forest Overlook. Go 1.4 mi. and turn right onto Hell Hollow Rd. (there is no sign here but two entrances). This road goes along the back of the reservoirs, crossing a few feeder streams. Walking along the road and these streams can be very productive in migration, although walking is difficult if you are not on a trail. Cooper's Hawk, Broad-winged Hawk, Hermit Thrush, Canada Warbler, Worm-eating Warbler, and Redstart can be found along this road in summer.

Directions. The entrance to Wild Creek Reservoir is the starting point of the tour. To reach the entrance, first follow directions in the site description for Beltzville State Park. From the main park entrance at Beltzville State Park, head east on Pohopoco Dr. 4.1 mi. Turn left at the sign into the entrance for Wild Creek Reservoir.

Notes. (1) The trails are not marked. It is best to obtain the 7.5 minute Pohopoco USGA quadrangle before doing extensive walking. **(2)** The area is patrolled by Bethlehem Water Supply personnel in green trucks with the city seal on the door. They are very cooperative and helpful. **(3)** There are sensitive nesting species in the area, especially raptors, so exercise good judgment if you come across one during the breeding season. **(4)** Restrooms are available at the Wild Creek overlook and the Penn Forest overlook. **(5)** There are rattlesnakes in the Hell Hollow Rd. area.

3. Little Gap

Description. Located on the Kittatinny Ridge, Little Gap is a good fall raptor-watching spot. Because it is located on the north side of the ridge, this site is best when westerly or northerly winds are present. This is especially true of the "rockpile" lookout which can be excellent on days with strong west or northwest winds. Birds tend to come through much closer here than at many of the other local hawk watch sites. The Blue Mountain ski area parking lot location has the advantage of being a "drive-up" lookout. No walking is necessary, and you have the option of watching on bitterly cold days from the protection of your car.

The gap sits within State Game Lands #168. The Appalachian Trail, which runs through the game lands, can be accessed from the gap and provides good woodland birding.

Birds. Raptors are the highlight of this site, but almost anything is possible during migration. One can bird the area in early morning for landbirds and then shift the focus to the raptors later in the morning and afternoon.

Breeding birds along the road to the ski area include Chestnut-sided, Prairie, and Worm-eating Warblers, Ovenbirds, and Indigo Buntings. Breeding birds within the game lands include Broad-winged Hawk, Whip-poor-will, Rose-breasted Grosbeak, and Yellow-billed and Black-billed Cuckoos.

Directions. From the intersection of Rt. 22 with Rt. 145 (MacArthur Rd.) in Whitehall, take Rt. 145 north for about 13 mi. to Walnutport. Turn right at Main St. (look for McDonald's on the left and Burger King on the right). This road becomes Mountain View Dr. and is also Rt. 946. Follow this road north about 4.3 mi., through Berlinsville to Danielsville. Turn left at the stoplight onto Blue Mountain Dr. Take Blue Mountain Dr. for 1.7 mi. and turn right at the sign for the Blue Mountain Ski Area. From here, there are two options for hawk-watching: 1) Go 0.3 mi. to a dirt road with a gate on the right and park there. Walk this road, which takes you up to the rockpiles located adjacent to the radio towers; or 2) Drive farther on through the gate to the large parking area, and watch for raptors from there. Note the gate closure times on the sign at the gate unless you plan on spending the night there!

There is also a third option that involves a longer hike. Another rockpile with a 360-degree view can be reached by parking on Blue Mountain Dr. at the Appalachian Trail sign (just south of the "Blue Mountain Ski Area" sign) and walking west toward the high-tension towers. Watch for the large rockpile on the left atop the mountain.

Note. The entire Kittatinny Ridge has been designated as an Important Bird Area (IBA) by Pennsylvania Audubon Society.

4. Lehigh River

Description. The Lehigh River, originating in the vicinity of Wilkes-Barre, passes through the Kittatinny Ridge at the Lehigh Gap. It runs roughly north-south through the Lehigh Valley until reaching Allentown. It then flows roughly west-east until it merges with the Delaware River in Easton. The historic Lehigh Canal runs the length of the river within the Lehigh Valley area.

Birds. Wooded and brushy areas along the river and canal banks provide good habitat for passerines. The water attracts herons, gulls, ducks, grebes, and other water birds. See descriptions for the sites named below for more on the birds.

Directions. A number of parks and public access areas provide good observation points. For directions, see site descriptions for the following areas: Hugh Moore Park, Lehigh Mountain Uplands, Riverview Park, Sand Island, Walnutport Area, and Whitehall Parkway and Ironton Rail Trail/D & L Trail.

5. Walnutport Area

Description. The Borough of Walnutport itself is mostly developed, but there are extensive natural areas along the Lehigh River both in town and north through Lehigh Gap. A section of the Lehigh Canal that runs the length of Walnutport is an easily-accessed public recreation area. Its tall sycamores and swampy woods offer excellent birding. Lehigh Gap, a complete break in the Kittatinny Ridge through which the river flows, is a diverse area including lowland groves, open thickets, small wetlands, dry woods, and rocky slopes. The abundant habitat provides for good year-round birding.

Birds. To visit the Lehigh Canal area, park in the first lot south of Main St. (see **Directions**). The sycamores there are excellent for Warbling Vireos in May. Walk south from the lot on the trail along the canal in spring or fall; migrant passerines use the woods to the right. Vireos, waxwings, warblers, orioles, and others are often present. Watch the opposite side of the canal for sparrows. Between the first and second canal lock you will see a nature trail on the right. Walking it provides access to a swampy area with tall trees. The river, on the other side of the woods, can be productive in the colder months. Try the canal north of Main St., too, which is accessed from the parking lot by crossing the road to a path.

To visit Lehigh Gap, park in the Appalachian Trail parking lot (see **Directions**). From the parking lot, there are two options: 1) the Appalachian Trail itself through the woods to the mountainside (and the summit); and 2) a level path heading toward Palmerton. The trail option provides a chance at many mixed woods species. Early summer is probably best. At this season, Prairie Warblers can be found in the semi-open area near the parking lot. Other summer residents of the dry oak/maple/hemlock woods along the Kittatinny Ridge include Broad-winged Hawks, Yellow-billed Cuckoos, and various flycatchers, warblers, and other passerines. Listen for Whip-poor-will at dawn or dusk; this very local species has been seen and heard nearby in early summer. Permanent residents in the area include Ruffed Grouse, Wild Turkey, Eastern Screech-Owl and Great Horned Owl, and Pileated Woodpecker. Migration augments the local population with many other songbirds, particularly thrushes and warblers. Winter is generally quiet, but listen for kinglets in March. In the spring, the rocky summit is a good place to view migrating raptors on days of southerly winds. The hike is steep and somewhat difficult.

The second option, the level path straight ahead (which may be somewhat overgrown with vegetation in summer), provides great scenery and a good chance for overhead raptors in season. Black Vultures are possible in the warmer months, and Rock Doves can be seen roosting in their natural habitat on a large crag to the right. After about 1.5 miles, you will come to a guardhouse at Aquashicola Creek. Bear left around the parking area there and walk through a small meadow to the water. Going under the highway bridge provides access to the entire greenbelt along the Lehigh River. Try crossing the creek on a railroad bridge there and walking along side the tracks north until they curve to the right under an overpass. A large cattail/Phragmites marsh will appear through the trees on the left; this area looks promising for wetland breeders. Also try walking along the river itself after crossing the creek. Gravel openings and a cinder path provide easy access to thickets that are undoubtedly excellent for migrants. When the river is low, small islands can also be explored. The full birding potential of this area has yet to be discovered. For starters, watch for waders, Osprey, and Spotted Sandpiper in summer, and check for waterfowl and raptors in the winter.

Directions. To reach the Lehigh Canal area, from the intersection of Rt. 22 with Rt. 145 (MacArthur Rd.) in Whitehall, take Rt. 145 north for about 13 mi. to Walnutport. Turn left onto Main St. (Rt. 946; look for McDonald's on the left and Burger King on the right). Proceed 0.6 mi. through town, driving carefully to avoid a speed trap. After crossing the canal, turn left on Lehigh St., just before the river. You will immediately come to the main parking area on the right. The canal can also be accessed from N. and S. Canal St., just before crossing the canal on Main St.

To reach Lehigh Gap, follow directions above to the intersection of Rt. 145 and Main St. (Rt. 946). From this point, continue on Rt. 145 north for about 1.8 mi. to where it ends at Rt. 248. Go east (right) and then almost immediately left on the first dirt road (which is small and almost hidden). Drive the short road, which is quite rough, up a hill to a large dirt parking area. This is the parking lot for the Appalachian Trail.

Notes. (1) The nearest restrooms are at fast food restaurants at the intersection of Rts. 145 and 946. (2) Hunting is allowed near Lehigh Gap; use caution in open seasons. (3) Along the Lehigh River, allow fishermen and dirt-bikers to have the right of way. (4) Do not, under any circumstance, cross over the concrete dividers into the large parking area at Aquashicola Creek. The outhouse and pay phone there are not for public use, and the lot itself is private property. Security personnel in the guardhouse may interfere if you trespass. (5) The Lehigh Canal is a popular recreation area. Arrive early, and respect the rights of joggers, bikers, fishermen, and people walking their pets. (6) The canal is wheelchair accessible. The Appalachian Trail is not, but the level path toward Palmerton is, for at least part of the way.

6. Lehigh Furnace Gap

Description. Lehigh Furnace Gap is a forested area bisected by a powerline cut atop the Kittatinny Ridge in northern Lehigh County. Rock outcroppings along the cut provide views to the north and south of the mountain.

Birds. Furnace Gap is best during spring and fall migration, for both songbirds and raptors. Fall raptor migration is best on days of northerly winds; west winds are not productive here. Spring raptors are only seen in numbers on days of southerly winds. Far fewer raptors are seen in spring compared to fall throughout this region, but perfect conditions here (south winds and cloud cover) during mid-to-late April can produce flights rivaling the best fall days. The power line cut is a convenient place to view most migrating songbirds in spring and fall, and Prairie Warbler nests along the cut.

Directions. From the intersection of Rt. 22 with Rt. 100 in Fogelsville, take Rt. 100 north 8.4 mi. to the intersection with Rt. 309. Turn left onto Rt. 309 and follow it 2.6 mi. to where it intersects with Rt. 143. From this point, continue on Rt. 309 another 2.0 mi. and turn right (east) on Mountain Rd. Follow Mountain Rd. for 5.2 mi. and turn left on Furnace Rd. Follow Furnace Rd. about 2 mi. to the top of the mountain and park off the road at any of several small cutouts near the communications tower. (Furnace Rd. becomes a dirt road with several intersections. To reach the top, always follow the road that continues uphill. There are two steep hairpin turns.) For fall raptors, climb the rocks under the power line on the west side of the road for a view to the north. For spring raptors, walk up the dirt road under the power lines on the east side of Furnace Rd until you have a good view to the south and west. There are additional lookouts along the ridge on either side of the road, reached by following the Appalachian Trail or unmarked trails.

Notes. (1) After a snowy winter, the road may be impassable well into March, but otherwise it is not difficult for two-wheel drive vehicles. (2) There are no restrooms. (3) There have been occasional reports of car vandalism at the parking areas. This is a fairly remote area and it is not recommended that birders visit alone. (4) The entire Kittatinny Ridge has been designated as an Important Bird Area (IBA) by Pennsylvania Audubon Society.

7. Bake Oven Knob

Description. Bake Oven Knob is a prominent feature on the Kittatinny Ridge. Three major rock outcroppings provide excellent lookout sites for hawk watching. They are reached on foot via a short section of the Appalachian Trail. The surrounding forest is oak-dominated mixed hardwood.

Birds. Resident birds include the common hardwood forest birds. Since there is a fairly large, unbroken tract of forest, such species as Scarlet Tanager and Pileated Woodpecker are seen regularly. Downy, Hairy, and (infrequently) Red-headed Woodpeckers can be seen along with Northern Flickers. Wild Turkeys and Ruffed Grouse are also present. During spring and fall migration, warblers and thrushes are commonly seen, with Hermit Thrushes regular in migration. A good variety of warblers, vireos, thrushes, and flycatchers is possible at these times, but not in the abundance typical of some other Lehigh Valley sites. Raptors such as Red-tailed and Sharp-shinned Hawks can be observed during the summer months along with both Turkey and Black Vultures, often seen soaring close to or below the South Lookout.

The biggest attraction of the Knob is the fall raptor migration, with 16 species (including the vultures) seen regularly. In mid-September, the most abundant raptor is the Broad-winged Hawk. The Sharp-shinned Hawk is the most abundant migrant during the first three weeks of October. By late October, the Red-tailed Hawk takes over as most abundant through the end of the season.

Bald and Golden Eagles are a major attraction, with dozens of each sighted each fall. Bald Eagles are most commonly seen in September and again in November, with Golden Eagles appearing in late October and November. Osprey and American Kestrels are common in September. Merlins and Peregrine Falcons are seen in relatively small numbers, mostly in early to mid-October. Red-shouldered Hawks are most commonly seen in the last three weeks of October and the first week of November. Cooper's Hawks are most often sighted from late September to early November, while Northern Goshawks are most common in November. Northern Harriers have the longest migration period, stretching throughout the entire fall season, with immatures and females more common earlier and males more common in November. Rough-legged Hawks are the least common migrant, with one or two seen on average in November. Occasionally an errant Swainson's Hawk may show up, or rarely a Gyrfalcon.

Loons, cormorants, Great Blue Herons, geese, swans, shorebirds, Ruby-throated Hummingbirds, and Common Ravens are also seen regularly from the lookouts. Chimney Swifts, swallows, Cedar Waxwings, Blue Jays and mixed flocks of blackbirds are also seen migrating. Monarch Butterflies are also seen heading for wintering grounds in Mexico. Late in the season, winter finches are often present, and Snow Buntings are sighted each year.

The South Lookout, at 1560 feet elevation, offers an impressive view of the Lehigh Valley area as well as an unobstructed view up ridge to the northeast. The lookout drops off abruptly, often providing views of soaring raptors from above. This lookout is used on days with either no wind or easterly or southerly winds to observe the fall hawk migration. To reach this lookout, find the trail head at the southeast corner of the parking lot. Walk along the trail (marked with white blazes on the trees) for 0.4 miles. This very rocky trail climbs steadily as it follows the ridge top. When the trail suddenly becomes steeper next to a rock slide, then levels off at the highest point on the ridge, you will see an old concrete foundation. On the left is the auxiliary North Lookout, a jumble of boulders with a rather restricted view of the ridge-and-valley province to the north. On the right, about 25 yards away, is the South Lookout.

On westerly or northerly winds, hawks are usually flying along the north side of the ridge. The main North Lookout is the preferred observation point on these days. To reach this lookout, continue on the trail from the vicinity of the South Lookout straight past the concrete foundation another 0.1 mile. The trail is very rocky as it heads gradually downhill. The main North Lookout is the pile of boulders just east through the trees. Climb over the top of the boulders to the front of the lookout, or skirt the lookout to the north following the blazes on the rocks for about 75 feet, then climb up the side of the North Lookout. From here, you can see both sides of the ridge but cannot look directly down on the forest canopy below.

Directions. From the intersection of Rt. 22 or I-78 with Rt. 100 in Fogelsville, take Rt. 100 north 8.2 mi. to the stop sign at the T intersection with Rt. 309. Turn right onto Rt. 309. In just 0.2 mi., turn left (toward Germansville) onto Bake Oven Rd. (There is a large house with pillars on the left corner.) Follow Bake Oven Rd. approximately 4.3 mi., through the stop sign at Mountain Rd., to a stop sign at Church Rd. Turn left to continue on Bake Oven Rd. for 0.2 mi. to the intersection with Walter Rd. Bear right to remain on Bake Oven Rd., which turns into a gravel road and shortly begins to go up the ridge. Continue 1.7 mi. to the parking lot, which is on the right at the crest of the ridge. The trail head is at the far end of the parking lot.

Notes. (1) Sturdy hiking boots are advised due to the rocky trails. This site, especially between the South Lookout and the main North Lookout, is not recommended for those who are unsteady on their feet. (2) The parking lot, trail, and lookouts are located on State Game Lands. Use caution during hunting seasons. (3) The road to the top of the ridge is sometimes rough and is not plowed or cindered in winter. (4) This is an undeveloped site with no restrooms or other facilities. (5) Spotting scopes are difficult to use here and are more practical if gunstock mounted for hand-held viewing. (6) Raptors can be seen at any time during daylight hours, with wide variation depending on weather conditions. On average, the hours from 10 a.m. to noon EST are typically the most productive. (7) Black Bears have occasionally been reported along the trail. (8) There have been occasional reports of vandalism of cars in the parking lot, so keep valuables hidden. This is a fairly remote site, and it is not advised to bird here alone. However, on fall weekends, other hikers and birders are likely to be present. (9) Contact the Wildlife Information Center for information about the Autumn Hawk Count conducted annually at Bake Oven Knob: P.O. Box 198, Slatington, PA 18080; (610) 760-8889. (10) The entire Kittatinny Ridge has been designated as an Important Bird Area (IBA) by Pennsylvania Audubon Society.

8. Bear Rocks

Description. Bear Rocks (also spelled Baer Rocks) is a large outcropping of boulders on the spine of the Kittatinny Ridge, 1.4 miles west of the Bake Oven Knob parking lot. This lookout offers a 360-degree view, making the site good for both spring and fall hawk migrations. It provides a view of Lehigh County and South Mountain to the south and the ridge-and-valley province of Schuylkill and Carbon Counties to the north, as well as a view up and down the ridge. It is surrounded by a stand of old-growth Eastern Hemlock, endangered by an insect infestation.

Birds. The description for Bake Oven Knob applies equally to Bear Rocks, except for the greater likelihood of finding kinglets and some warblers in the hemlocks. The hawk flight can be higher above the ridge than at Bake Oven Knob, but the view to the south and west makes Bear Rocks an excellent spring hawk watch site.

Directions. See directions to the parking lot for Bake Oven Knob. Pass this lot and look for a second lot, on the left, very shortly after the first. The lookout is about a 40-minute hike from the parking lot. Find the Appalachian Trail at the southwest corner of the lot, and follow it west. The trail here is an old logging road and is easy, flat walking. Take the left fork when the road splits, still following the white blazes of the Appalachian Trail. The road eventually gives way to a rocky trail. Continue to the point where the trail makes a fairly sharp left turn, as noted by the double blaze on a tree. At this point, leave the trail and bushwhack straight ahead to the stand of large hemlock trees that obscures the boulder pile. Climb to the top of the boulders to reach the viewing area. This is a short but very steep climb.

Notes. (1) The trail and lookout are State Game Lands, and hunting occurs during the regular seasons. **(2)** See the Bake Oven Knob site description for other notes. **(3)** The entire Kittatinny Ridge has been designated as an Important Bird Area (IBA) by Pennsylvania Audubon Society.

9. Leaser Lake Recreation Area

Description. Leaser Lake is a 117-acre PA Fish Commission lake located in Lynn Township, Lehigh County. The area east, west, and south of the lake is mostly farmland. The steep, wooded slopes of the Kittatinny Ridge abut the north side of the lake.

Birds. The lake itself is good for loons, grebes, waterfowl, and swallows in the proper season. The shoreline is generally not good for shorebirds because of the amount of rock and shale present. However, small numbers of shorebirds are occasionally seen. The wooded areas surrounding the lake throughout the recreation area hold many breeding and migrating woodland birds, including some at the higher elevations not commonly found elsewhere. The farm fields and ponds adjacent to the area provide good habitat for grassland and wading birds.

A good place to begin a trip to this area is at the north parking lot. From here, there is a good view of the water surface. Acadian Flycatchers breed in the hemlocks on the north side of the lake just before the north parking lot. The trees along the roadside in both directions from the north parking lot can also be productive for migrating warblers, vireos, and other songbirds.

For less common breeding warblers along with other woodland birds, turn left out of the north parking lot and continue on Ontelaunee Rd. 0.6 mi. At the intersection with Springhouse Rd., bear left onto Springhouse Rd. In another 0.5 mi., at the stop sign, turn right onto Leaser Rd. Park in one of several turnoffs just past this point and walk uphill to the top of the mountain. Breeding Cerulean, Worm-eating, Hooded, and Kentucky Warblers can be found in trees along the roadside.

Heading back downhill from the parking turnoffs, both Leaser Rd. and the unmarked third road at this intersection (Blue Mountain House Rd.) provide good birding. On Blue Mountain House Rd., check ponds along the roadside. At 1.8 mi. down this road, continue past the intersection with Slateville Rd. and check the fields for breeding grassland birds such as Bobolinks, Eastern Meadowlarks, and Vesper, Savannah, and Grasshopper Sparrows. Leaser Rd. likewise provides good grassland birding. Utt Rd., which runs between Leaser Rd. and Slateville Rd., also has ponds and fields good for birds. A Willow Flycatcher can often be found in brushy areas along this road.

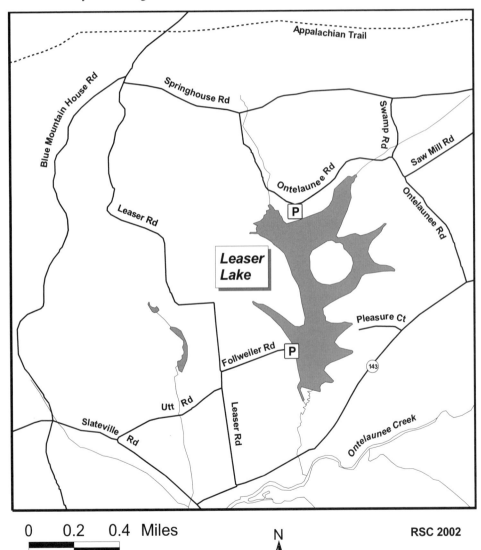

0   0.2   0.4 Miles   N   RSC 2002

Follweiller Rd. off of Leaser Rd. provides access to the west parking area of the lake and a view of water areas not visible from the north lot.

After becoming familiar with the above areas, birders may wish to begin trips by birding back roads into the lake. Instead of taking Rt. 143 directly to Ontelaunee Rd., from the intersection of Rt. 309 with Rt. 143, follow Rt. 143 only 2.0 mi. and turn right onto Gun Club Rd. Take Gun Club Rd. 0.9 mi. and turn left onto Fort Everett Rd. At 0.1 mi. on Fort Everett Rd., check the pond on the left for herons, shorebirds, and warblers, and surrounding fields for grassland birds. Continue on Fort Everett Rd., listening in the vicinity of hemlocks 0.6 mi. further for Pine and other warblers during migration. Another 1.4 mi. farther, turn right onto Springhouse Rd. About 0.5 mi. down Springhouse Rd., a white barn sits near a wet grassy area that may produce herons, Snipe, and swallows. Check the nearby fields for Bobolink and Meadowlarks. In about another 0.5 mi., turn right onto Behler Rd. and then, in 0.3 mi., turn left onto Sawmill Rd. Take Sawmill Rd. 0.5 mi. to Ontelaunee Rd. and turn right. Bear left very shortly at the brown sign to stay on Ontelaunee and reach the north parking lot. (The dirt road bearing right also provides good birding).

Directions. From the intersection of Rt. 22 with Rt. 100 in Fogelsville, take Rt. 100 north 8.2 mi. to the intersection with Rt. 309. Turn left onto Rt. 309 and follow it 2.6 mi. to where it intersects with Rt. 143. Turn left onto Rt. 143. Take Rt. 143 for 4.7 mi. to Ontelaunee Rd. and turn right onto Ontelaunee. Follow Ontelaunee about 1 mi. to the north parking lot. (At the brown sign at 0.7 mi., bear left to stay on Ontelaunee). See the preceding paragraph for an alternative approach through back roads.

Notes. (1) Leaser Lake is popular for fishing and picnicking in warm weather, so arrive early if you want to see waterfowl. **(2)** A scope is helpful. **(3)** There are outhouses at the parking lots on the north, east, and west sides of the lake. **(4)** There is a general store in the village of Wanamakers, on Rt. 143 west of Ontelaunee Rd. by 1.5 mi., where birders can buy refreshments (not open Sundays). **(5)** The entire Kittatinny Ridge has been designated as an Important Bird Area (IBA) by Pennsylvania Audubon Society.

10. Mount Bethel Fens

Description. The Mount Bethel Fens, located in northern Northampton County, are wetlands that were created by glaciers moving over limestone bedrock. The water that percolates to the surface has a high lime content, creating calcareous fens. The alkaline, water-soaked peat that forms its soil supports a number of plants unique to these fens, many of which are rare or endangered. The fens are interspersed through diverse habitats including free-flowing stream, beaver pond, marsh, deciduous woodlands, and meadow. The Nature Conservancy considers this site to be the most important natural area in the Lehigh-Northampton Counties area.

Some of the area is owned by The Nature Conservancy. Another segment belongs to Eastern Industries, and the rest is private land.

Birds. Because of the wide range of adjacent habitats, the birdlife associated with these fens is varied. The body of water created by a beaver dam and the surrounding marsh produces water birds of many kinds. Ducks, geese, rails, herons, gulls, and swallows all may be seen. A variety of songbirds occur in migration, including warblers, vireos, thrushes, and flycatchers, many of which also breed here. The abundant Black Willow trees near the stream and beaver pond usually have nesting Warbling Vireos. Woodpeckers, including Pileated, are seen regularly. Wild Turkeys, Ruffed Grouse, American Woodcock, and Snipe occur. Red-tailed, Sharp-shinned, and Cooper's Hawks are present in all seasons. Turkey and Black Vultures are flyovers, and Bald Eagles are occasionally seen due to the proximity of the Delaware River and Lake Minsi. Fish Crows are as common as American Crows. Grassy and brushy areas are good for sparrows, including Song and Swamp Sparrows, which breed here. White-throated, Fox, and Tree Sparrows are found seasonally. Scattered sand and gravel pits provide open areas where shorebirds and herons are often seen.

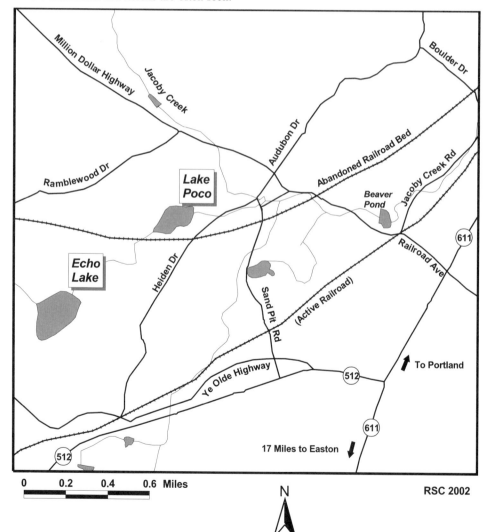

0   0.2   0.4   0.6 Miles

N

RSC 2002

Directions. From the intersection of Rt. 22 with Rt. 512, take Rt. 22 east approximately 10.5 mi. to the 4th St. exit in Easton. From the end of the 4th St. exit ramp, turn left and follow the signs to Rt. 611 north. Take Rt. 611 north 7.2 mi. to the stop light in the town of Martins Creek. Make a right to stay on 611. One mi. farther, at the intersection with Martins Creek-Belvidere Hwy., bear left to continue on Rt. 611. Follow Rt. 611 approximately 9.3 mi. farther into the town of Mt. Bethel and turn left onto Railroad Ave. at TK's Restaurant. At about 0.3 mi. on Railroad Ave., the road intersects with the Million Dollar Highway to the left and Jacoby Creek Rd. to the right. Explore along Jacoby Creek Rd. to the railway substation, the Million Dollar Highway up to Heiden Dr./Audubon Rd. (about a mile), and Sand Pit Rd. (turn left from the Million Dollar Highway shortly before reaching Heiden Dr./Audubon Rd.).

Notes. (1) The roads in this area have little traffic. One can pull to the side and walk along the roadside. **(2)** Avoid trespassing on portions of the fens marked as private.

11. Minsi Lake Recreational Area, Bear Swamp Recreational Area, and East Bangor Dam

Description. Minsi Lake Recreational Area is a Northampton County park located at the base of the Kittatinny Ridge, just north of the town of Bangor. It is a multi-use area consisting of a 117-acre man-made lake with nature trails around it. To the west of the lake is Bear Swamp Recreational Area, which has an archery complex and several trails. The trails cover a variety of habitats ranging from mixed oak-maple woodland to sphagnum swamp. East Bangor Dam contains similar habitat but is only lightly used for recreational purposes. The upper section consists of shallow, largely undisturbed wetlands.

Birds. Access to Minsi Lake is by two parking lots, one on the east and one on the west edge. A wooded hiking trail runs between the two lots and there is a side trail that leads to the midpoint of the lake. This trail is good for migrant warblers, vireos, thrushes, orioles and tanagers, some of which also nest during the summer months. Pileated Woodpeckers and Wild Turkeys are found here.

Both Minsi Lake and East Bangor Dam are good for migrating waterfowl, Osprey, and swallows. East Bangor Dam is home to nesting Wood Ducks, Mute Swans, and Purple Martins. Great Blue Herons commonly roost there.

The boardwalk trail, the feature attraction of Bear Swamp, is a raised trail through a small section of a sphagnum swamp that covers an extensive area on both sides of the road at the archery complex. There is also a small pond and interpretive area at the entrance to the trail. Access to this trail is by parking at the archery target range. Cross the road, walk west (left) along an old railroad bed for 100 yards, then take the second right just before the stone row. Cross the gravel area and go to the right of the short wooden walkway (which leads to the interpretive building and pond) to reach the path to the boardwalk. The trail makes almost a complete loop; at the end, to return to the starting point, walk to the left about 50-100 yards. Barred Owl, Pileated Woodpecker, Acadian Flycatcher, Wood Thrush, and Swamp Sparrow are some of the birds that nest in the swamp.

Directions. To reach the archery complex parking lot at Bear Swamp, from the intersection of Rt. 22 with Rt. 33, take Rt. 33 north for about 11 mi. to the Rt. 512 (Wind Gap) exit. Bear right at the end of the exit ramp and go north on Rt. 512 (towards Bangor) about 6.3 mi. to the intersection with Rt. 191. (Rt. 512 makes several abrupt turns; follow signs carefully.) Turn left onto Rt. 191 and follow it north about 2.4 mi. to the intersection with Lake Minsi Dr. Turn right onto Lake Minsi Dr. and follow it 1.3 mi. to the stop sign at the intersection with Creek Rd. Turn left on Creek Rd. (which is labeled Lake Minsi Dr. in places) and go 0.7 mi. to the parking lot on the right.

To reach the west entrance at Minsi Lake, go another 0.3 mi. on Creek Rd. and turn left at Blue Mountain Rd, then take an immediate right into the lot entrance. To reach the east entrance, return to Creek Rd./Lake Minsi Dr. and continue 0.3 mi. Turn left onto East Shore Dr. and proceed 0.5 mi. to the entrance.

To get to East Bangor Dam, return to Lake Minsi Dr. and turn left. Head south on Lake Minsi Dr. for 1.3 mi., then turn left at the stop sign onto Ridge Rd. Very shortly, go right at the 4-way stop onto Tott's Gap Rd. (also called Johnsonville Rd. in places). Take Tott's Gap Rd. 0.7 mi. and turn right at the stop sign onto Rt. 512 (Mt. Bethel Highway). Follow Rt. 512 for about 1.8 mi. (At 1.1 mi., look for the Purple Martin colony at the intersection with Reimer Rd. Where Rt. 512 makes a sharp right shortly thereafter, stay with it.) Turn right onto Broad St., and follow it 0.3 mi. down the hill and across the railroad tracks. There is a small parking area on the left side of Broad. In another 0.1 mi., turn right onto Lakewood Dr. to access the main parking area and boat launch.

Notes. (1) The park is open to the public from dawn until dusk daily. Guided nature walks are offered periodically, and additional walks can be arranged through the Northampton County parks office. **(2)** The parking areas at Minsi Lake have information boards with regulations, bird lists, and trail maps. Both lots have portable toilets. **(3)** Because the soil is poorly drained throughout the park, muddy conditions can exist at any time of year on the trails. **(4)** Black Bears occur in the swamp at the archery range at Minsi Lake.

12. Cherry Valley-Portland-Mt. Bethel Area

Description. This area includes parts of extreme southern Monroe County adjacent to the Northampton County line plus the northwest corner of Northampton County in Upper and Lower Mt. Bethel Townships. A driving tour through it provides access to a variety of habitats including small lakes, ponds, and swampy fields, the Delaware River, and open fields and hedgerows.

Birds. The ponds and lakes along Lower Cherry Valley and Poplar Valley roads are good for virtually all dabbling duck species, especially during March. Pied-billed Grebes are often seen as well. The meanders of Cherry Creek create an excellent swampy floodplain that is best in March and April and is noted for dabbling ducks (Blue-winged Teal, Green-winged Teal, Northern Pintail and Wood Duck), as well as Great Blue Herons, American Kestrels, Common

Snipe, Killdeer, Woodcock, and American Pipits. The drive and observation points along the Delaware River often provide views of Bald Eagle and many species of diving ducks including Bufflehead, Common Goldeneye, Common Merganser, and Ring-necked Duck in the spring. The turn-off to Slateford Farm is excellent for warblers during the spring. The fields around the Martins Creek power plant are good for sparrows and Snow Buntings in winter and early spring. Indigo Buntings and other field species are found in summer along with nesting Ospreys on the transmission towers and Warbling Vireos in the sycamores along the Delaware River.

The following provides a 30-mile driving tour through the area. To reach the starting point of the tour, see **Directions**.

From the starting point on Lower Cherry Valley Rd., Cherry Valley Center Lake is 0.8 mi. east, on the right, followed by several arms of Eastwood Farms Lake extending along the left. Both are good for all dabbling ducks and Pied-billed Grebes. Continue on Lower Cherry Valley Rd. another 4 mi. to a sign for the village of Kemmerton (Kemmererville). One-tenth of a mi. further, at the Y intersection, bear right onto Poplar Valley Rd. Follow Poplar Valley Rd. for 0.5 mi. and turn left onto Blakeslee Rd. Follow Blakeslee Rd. for 0.3 mi. and make a hard right at the stop sign onto Middle Rd. Follow Middle Rd. to the Y intersection at the farm. Bear left between the shed and the barn. You will immediately come to the swampy floodplain of Cherry Creek on the left. The entire floodplain is excellent for Great Blue Herons, dabbling ducks, shorebirds, and other water birds. It is the best birding spot on the tour.

Continue 0.8 mi. to the stop sign and turn right onto Cherry Valley Rd. Go 2.5 mi. on Cherry Valley Rd. to the junction of Rt. 191. Turn left onto Rt. 191 and in 0.2 mi. take the second right to continue on Cherry Valley Rd. Continue on Cherry Valley Rd. for 3.0 mi. to Rt. 611. Turn right on 611 South. You will come to two overlooks that are good for Bald Eagles in winter and early spring (Resort Point will be 0.5 mi. south on the left; Arrow Island is 2.5 mi. south on the left). After Arrow Island, remain on Rt. 611 South for another 0.9 mi. Turn right onto National Park Dr. at the Slateford Farmhouse sign. Go 0.5 mi. to the parking lot. This spot is excellent for warblers in spring.

Return to Rt. 611 and continue south for 1.8 mi. until you see the Duckloe Furniture sign on the left in the town of Portland. A footbridge crosses the Delaware River here. This is an excellent spot for diving ducks in winter and early spring. Continue south on Rt. 611 for 4.8 mi. (bear right after the light at State St. to remain on 611, and proceed through the towns of Mount Bethel and Stone Church). Turn left onto Riverton Rd. and proceed 3.5 mi. Several small pulloffs to the right along this road provide good Delaware River viewing areas for diving ducks as well.

At the T intersection at the end of Riverton Rd., turn right onto the Martins Creek-Belvidere Hwy. and continue 2.6 mi. to the PP&L Martins Creek Steam Electric Station. (You will pass the Martins Creek hiking trails; see the Martins Creek Environmental Preserve site description). An Osprey nest can be seen on one of the high tension line towers as you approach the power plant on the left. Turn left into the power plant onto Foul Rift-Depues

Ferry Rd at the PP&L Martins Creek sign. One or more fly ash basins (depending on current use) may be seen along this road; they are good for waterfowl. Follow Foul Rift-Depues Ferry Rd. 0.6 mi. and turn right onto the continuation of Depues Ferry Rd. (look for the Martins Creek Steam Electric Station sign.) Watch the brushy area on the left for White-crowned and American Tree Sparrows in winter. Continue 0.8 mi. on Depues Ferry Rd. to the sign for the PP&L Martins Creek boat access area. Bear left at the sign and go 0.1 mi. to the boat access. A railroad trestle crosses the river and is a good lookout for diving ducks in winter and Warbling Vireos in summer.

Directions. To reach the starting point of the tour, from the intersection of Rt. 22 with Rt. 33, take Rt. 33 north 16.6 mi. to the Saylorsburg exit. From the exit, turn right onto Cherry Valley Rd. Follow Cherry Valley Rd. 0.3 mi. to the stop sign and turn left onto Hamilton South. Follow Hamilton South for 0.7 mi. to the Cherry Valley Vineyards sign. Turn left onto Lower Cherry Valley Rd.

Notes. (1) Much of the land along this route consists of private property, so birding should be done from the road, pulloffs, and observation points. Exceptions are in the vicinity of the Delaware Water Gap National Recreation Area and public areas of the PP&L land. Heed "no trespassing" signs on PP&L land. **(2)** The entire route takes approximately 2.5 hours at a leisurely birding pace. **(3)** The northernmost portion of this tour extends just beyond the border of our coverage circle, and sightings records from this portion are therefore not included in book. This portion is included in the tour to provide a complete semi-circular driving route through this excellent region.

13. Smith Gap and Vicinity

Description. Located on the south side of the Kittatinny Ridge, Smith Gap Rd. is a part-paved, part-gravel road that crosses over the ridge at Smith Gap. This road allows birding at all elevations of the steeply-wooded slopes of the mountain. Skunk Rd. passes through the woodlands at the base of the mountain. Moore Appalachian Park, an undeveloped park used mostly for horseback riding, is located along Skunk Rd. A State Game Lands planting area is located nearby on Mountain Rd.

Birds. The Smith Gap area is best during the breeding season for birds not easily found elsewhere in our area. The following provides a tour covering a range of elevations. To reach the starting point of the tour, see **Directions**.

From the intersection of Smith Gap Rd. with Skunk Rd., head up the mountain on Smith Gap Rd. About halfway to the top, Smith Gap Rd. turns sharply to the left. There is a wide pulloff at this turn. Park here and bird up and down the road. Breeding birds here have included Great-crested Flycatchers, Yellow-throated Vireos, Blue-gray Gnatcatchers, Cerulean, Worm-eating, and Black-and-White Warblers, Northern Parulas, and Indigo Buntings. Winter Wren has been heard here in early summer.

Farther up the road is a Game Lands parking lot on the left where the road makes a sharp turn to the left. Park here and bird the upper section of the mountainside. To bird the base of the mountain, head back downhill and take the first left onto Skunk Rd. You can bird all along this road. Moore Appalachian Park is located 0.6 mi. down Skunk Rd. Breeding birds in this area include Pileated Woodpecker and, sometimes, Kentucky Warbler.

Continue down Skunk Rd. to where it intersects with Mountain Rd. and turn right. Another good birding spot is the Game Lands planting area, located 0.4 mi. down this road. Park in the small lot located on the right just past the Game Lands sign. Here, you can bird the areas on both sides of the road. The area across the road from the sign contains several habitats including a wooded stream, two small ponds, areas of second-growth, and small fields with hedgerows. Continue on Mountain Rd. to the next intersection, which is Smith Gap Rd. From here, turn right to head back up the mountain or turn left to head back to Klecknersville.

Directions. To reach the starting point of the tour, from the intersection of Rt. 22 with Rt. 987 (Airport Rd.), take Rt. 987 north 10.6 mi. to Klecknersville. (Rt. 987 makes several sharp turns; follow signs carefully.) Continue straight (west) onto Rt. 946 (Mountain View Dr.). In 0.3 mi., just past the Klecknersville firehouse, turn right onto Point Phillips Rd. and follow this road for about 1.7 mi. Where the road makes a sharp bend to the right and becomes Scenic Dr., go left instead onto Smith Gap Rd. At 0.2 mi. on Smith Gap Rd., be sure to bear left at the Y intersection to stay on this road. Continue on Smith Gap Rd. another 1.6 mi. to the intersection with Skunk Rd., which is located at the base of the ridge.

Note. The entire Kittatinny Ridge has been designated as an Important Bird Area (IBA) by Pennsylvania Audubon Society.

14. Graver's Hill

Description. Graver's Hill is a large expanse of open cultivated fields. Crops vary from year to year but usually include corn, soybeans, and winter wheat.

Birds. In summer, the fields are a good place to locate sparrow species such as Vesper, Grasshopper, Field, and Savannah. Horned Larks have bred here. The fields on the east side of Delps Rd., about halfway between S. Oak and Point Phillips Rds., are usually a reliable summertime location for Bobolinks.

In winter, after the crops are harvested, these fields may be the best place in northern Northampton County to view Horned Larks and Snow Buntings, and occasionally Lapland Longspurs. Northern Harriers are sighted regularly, and American Pipits are possible.

Directions. From the intersection of Rt. 22 with Rt. 987 (Airport Rd.), take Rt. 987 north 10.6 mi. to Klecknersville. (Rt. 987 makes several sharp turns; follow signs carefully.) Continue straight (west) onto Rt. 946 (Mountain View Dr.). In 0.3 mi., just past the Klecknersville firehouse, turn right onto Point Phillips Rd. One hundred feet later, turn left onto Delps Rd. (the sign is hidden on the right). Follow this road for 0.9 mi. to S. Oaks Rd. and turn left onto S. Oaks Rd. (a gravel road). Park along this road. Although narrow, there is very little traffic.

Notes. (1) Scanning the fields east of Delps Rd. should be done on foot. Leave your vehicle parked on S. Oaks Rd. **(2)** The fields are private property, and all birding should be done from the roadways. **(3)** A spotting scope is recommended. **(4)** In spring and summer, a trip to Graver's Hill can be combined with a visit to the Smith Gap site to add a good variety of woodland birds.

15. Jacobsburg State Park

Description. This 1,168-acre Northampton County park is mostly undeveloped. Its 18.5 miles of trails cover habitats including mature forests of hemlock and oak, coniferous forests, undeveloped fields in various stages of growth, and areas of wetlands.

Birds. Across the road and slightly west of the main parking area is a bird blind and a recently constructed hummingbird garden. Feeders at the blind are maintained in winter and attract a variety of woodland birds. Check the garden for hummingbirds in the warmer months.

The 1.9 mile Henry's Woods trail passes through outcroppings of slate and large stands of mature hemlock and white oak, with the Bushkill Creek below. Many songbirds nest or migrate through this area, as well as Great Horned Owl and occasional ducks and shorebirds along the creek. Louisiana Waterthrushes can often be found along the creek in migration. The hemlock woods are particularly good for thrushes and woodpeckers.

The Homestead Trail above Henry's Woods meanders for about 2.8 miles through fields and woods. The fields hold a variety of grassland sparrows. This area can also be excellent for migrating warblers in early to late spring, featuring all of the more commonly found species along with Prairie and Wilson's Warblers and Yellow-Breasted Chat. Eastern Bluebirds have also been known to nest here.

Sober's Run, named for the little tributary of the Bushkill Creek that runs through it, is in the northwest portion of the park (parking is off Belfast Rd. about 0.75 mi. past the park office). It offers a tranquil area where the trail winds through evergreen woods and eventually through grassy fields. Hawks are often seen over the fields. In migration, the woods hold vireos, many species of warblers, thrushes (including Veery), Scarlet Tanagers, and orioles, some of which also nest there.

Other trails throughout the park offer good birding through a variety of habitats. Some, such as the Toth Ridge Trail, involve uneven ground and somewhat difficult footing.

Directions. From the intersection of Rt. 22 with Rt. 33, take Rt. 33 north 7.0 mi. to the Belfast exit. At the end of the exit, turn right, go to the next stop sign, and turn left onto Belfast

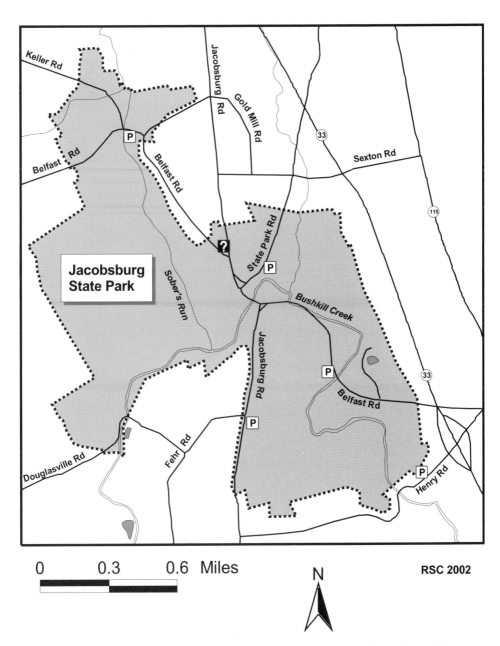

0   0.3   0.6 Miles   N   **RSC 2002**

Rd. The main parking area is about 0.5 mi. down the road. There are also other parking areas throughout the park, including one on Henry Rd. that is open from 8:30 a.m. to 3:30 p.m., and others on Jacobsburg Rd. across from Fehr Rd., Douglasville Rd., and State Park Rd.

Notes. (1) The main parking area has an information board with a trail map of the park. Individual maps are usually available there. Maps may also be picked up at the park office located on Jacobsburg Rd. just past its intersection with Belfast Rd., about a mile beyond the main parking lot. **(2)** The office is open from 8:00 a.m. to 4:00 p.m., Monday through Friday. It has lists of park activities including bird and wildflower walks. For more information, call (610) 746-2801 or visit the park web site at <www.dcnr.state.pa.us/stateparks/parks/j-burg.htm>. **(3)** Outhouses are located just over the bridge from the main parking area, and at the lots on Henry Rd. and State Park Rd. **(4)** The park itself is open from sunrise to sunset. For birding, it is best to arrive early in the morning, since the park can become very crowded, especially on weekends. **(5)** Hunting is allowed in the park. The areas where hunting is allowed are clearly marked but caution must be used when visiting those areas during hunting seasons.

16. Albert Road Ponds

Description. The Albert Road ponds are three private ponds with shrubby and wooded surrounding areas and farm fields nearby.

Birds. The ponds can be excellent in late winter and early spring for migrating waterfowl. Many duck species have been seen, including Ruddy Duck, Pintail, Bufflehead, and Northern Shoveler as well as more common species. Common Loons and Snow Geese are also seen here. A variety of hawks, Wild Turkey, Ruffed Grouse, and passerines have been seen in the surrounding areas.

Directions. From the intersection of Rt. 22 with Rt. 33, take Rt. 33 north 7.0 mi. to the Belfast exit. At the end of the exit ramp, turn right, go to the stop sign, and turn right onto Belfast Rd. In just 0.1 mi., turn left onto Sullivan Trail Rd. Take Sullivan Trail Rd. 2.0 mi. and turn left onto State Park Rd. After 0.3 mi., turn right onto Albert Rd. The ponds are another 0.3 mi down Albert Rd. on the left.

Notes. (1) The ponds and surrounding areas are private property. Bird only from the roadside. **(2)** A scope is helpful.

17. Martins Creek Environmental Preserve

Description. The Martins Creek Environmental Preserve (also known as Tekening) is located along the Delaware River in Lower Mt. Bethel Twp., Northampton County, just north of PP&L's Martins Creek Steam Electric Station. The 223-acre site is owned and managed by PP&L and is open to the public. The preserve contains mostly mature deciduous woodlands with lush understory and occasional red cedars. There are also open fields and views of the river. There are about 5 miles of trails, with trailheads at both the north and south ends. The Blue Trail parallels the river, passing by Foul Rift, an area of whitewater rapids.

Birds. This area attracts warblers and other neotropical migrants, and it can be excellent in summer for nesting species such as Scarlet Tanager, Eastern Bluebird, warblers, and woodland hawks. The Delaware River in this vicinity can be good for waterfowl, particularly mergansers and Wood Ducks, and for river waders, especially Green Herons. All of these are commonly seen in the nesting season.

There are active Osprey nests on the large power line towers along Martins Creek-Belvidere Hwy. and on platforms near the south entrance to the area. Peregrine Falcons have also nested here. Other birds of prey -- such as Northern Harriers, American Kestrels, accipiters, and Broad-winged Hawks -- are found along this road and in the woods, as are owls. Blue Grosbeaks and a variety of sparrows make regular appearances on the road edges and in the fields in spring.

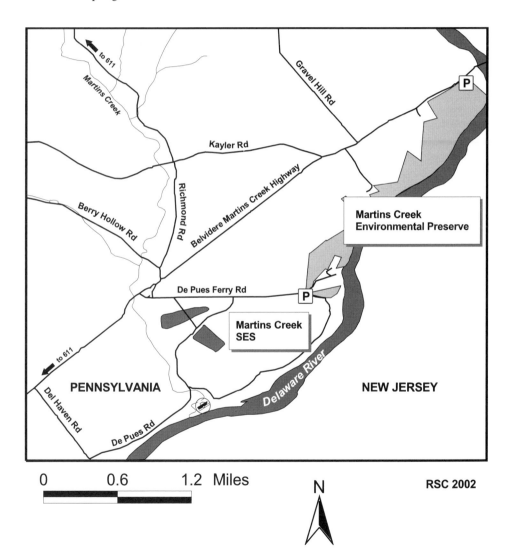

A productive loop for spring migrants, especially warblers, begins at the north parking lot. Take the Orange Trail (the first right off the trailhead) and follow it through woods and fields until a steep stairway on the left leads toward the river where you can pick up the Blue Trail back to the lot.

A feeding station located near the boat launch is worth a visit. It has had up to 40 White-crowned Sparrows in winter along with other visitors. The banks of the creek that flows through this area can also be very productive for migrants.

Directions. From the intersection of Rt. 22 with Rt. 512, take Rt. 22 east approximately 10.5 mi. to the 4th St. exit in Easton. From the end of the 4th St. exit ramp, turn left and follow the signs to Rt. 611 north. Take Rt. 611 north about 7.5 mi. (stopping, if desired, at two well-marked scenic lookouts along the way) to the stop light in the town of Martins Creek. Make a right to stay on 611. One mi. farther, at the intersection with Martins Creek-Belvidere Hwy., Rt. 611 bears left; instead, go straight onto Martins Creek-Belvidere Hwy. In 2.9 mi., turn right onto Foul Rift-Depues Ferry Rd at the PP&L Martins Creek sign. Proceed down Foul Rift-Depues Ferry Rd. and follow signs to the south parking area.

To reach the boat launch area, follow signs on Foul Rift-Depues Ferry Rd. before the south parking lot or see directions in the Cherry Valley-Portland-Mt. Bethel site description. The feeders are hidden in the brushy area just after the turn toward the boat launch.

To reach the north lot, drive another 2.3 mi. along Martins Creek-Belvidere Hwy. and look for the Tekening sign on the right.

Notes. (1) Food and restrooms are available in Belvidere, NJ, across the river. During the summer, an outhouse is available at the boat launch area. (2) Hunting is permitted in season.

18. Delaware River

Description. The Delaware River, originating in the Catskill Mountains of New York, flows the length of the Pennsylvania-New Jersey border before emptying into the Delaware Bay. The Delaware Canal is a narrow strip of slower-moving water along its western edge. Although some of the most scenic parts of the river are north of the Lehigh Valley area, its banks are undeveloped throughout much of the Valley, and points of access to the river provide good opportunities for viewing waterbirds.

Birds. The river attracts a variety of waterbirds including grebes, cormorants, gulls, and ducks, especially in winter. Its banks often provide good birding for woodland birds, especially in migration. See descriptions for the sites named below for more on the birds.

Directions. Rt. 611 parallels the river through the Lehigh Valley area and provides a large number of access points to the river. See the site description for Wy-Hit-Tuk Park for one location south of Rt. 22 that is accessed easily from I-78. More northern access points can be reached by taking Rt. 22 to the 4th St. exit in Easton and following signs to Rt. 611. From this point, heading north on 611, there is a scenic overlook 2.2 mi. north of Easton. Another opportunity for viewing the river is 2.8 mi. further on Rt. 611, at a well-marked parking lot and boat ramp called Sandts Eddy Boat Access. Farther north, Martins Creek Environmental Preserve has a trail that overlooks the river; see the site description for this area. See the Cherry Valley-Portland-Mt. Bethel Area site description for additional access north of Martins Creek.

19. Merrill Creek Reservoir and Environmental Preserve

Description. Situated on Scott's Mountain in Warren County, New Jersey, the 650-acre reservoir is surrounded by 2,000 acres of forest and fields. Two hundred and ninety acres along

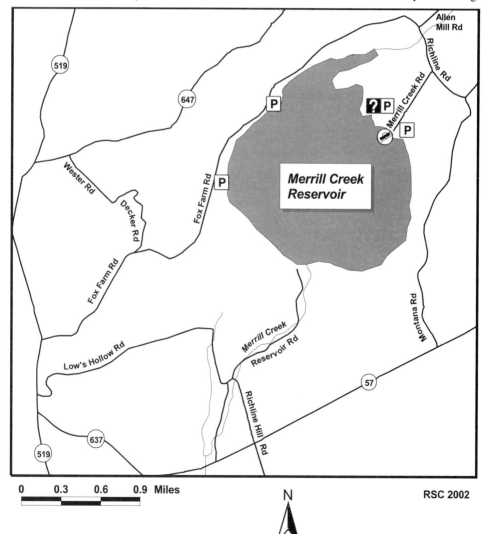

the shore of the reservoir are maintained as a wildlife preserve. A hiking trail runs along the perimeter of the reservoir and through wooded areas at its north end. There is an observation blind in the woods and several overlook areas for viewing the water surface.

Birds. Birds attracted to the water include Common Loons, grebes, Double-crested Cormorants, American Coots, and many species of waterfowl (28 species appear on the reservoir checklist). The variety is greatest during spring and fall migration, but some species are also present in winter. Bald Eagles are seen here, and Ruffed Grouse, Wild Turkey, and Pileated Woodpeckers are resident.

A good place to begin a visit is at the Visitors' Center. Feeders there attract woodland birds, sometimes including Pine Siskins in the winter. The center also provides a somewhat distant view of the water. Trail heads are near there, and the trails provide good birding through mainly deciduous forest. Good views of the water are available by foot from the Shoreline Trail and by car from two overlooks on the west side of the reservoir, off of Fox Farm Rd.

Fields off of Fox Farm Rd. provide habitat for Eastern Bluebirds, sparrows and other grassland birds, and hawks. The parking area at the south end of Fox Farm Rd. is a good spot from which to look for field birds.

Directions. From the intersection of Rt. 22 with Rt. 512 in Bethlehem, go east on Rt. 22 for 12.7 mi., into Phillipsburg, NJ, to where Rt. 57 splits off. Rt. 22 bears right; instead, go straight onto Rt. 57. Continue on Rt. 57 for 4.7 mi. to the stop sign at Montana Rd. Turn left onto Montana Rd. and follow it 2.1 mi. to the intersection with Richline Rd. Turn left onto Richline Rd. At 0.3 mi. on Richline, turn left onto Merrill Creek Rd. Another 0.3 mi. later, turn right into the Visitor Center entrance. The Center itself is another 0.3 mi.

Notes. (1) The Visitor Center contains educational exhibits and restrooms. Trail maps and a checklist are available there. The center is open 7 days a week, 8:30 a.m. to 4:30 p.m., except on major holidays. The phone number is (908) 454-1213. (2) A scope is needed for good looks at most birds on the water. One is provided for use from the Visitor Center viewing windows.

20. Hugh Moore Park

Description. Hugh Moore Park stretches narrowly along six miles of the Lehigh River, beginning at the confluence of the Delaware and Lehigh rivers and ending at the Bethlehem Boat Club at Hope Rd. in Bethlehem. The park runs along both the north and south banks of the Lehigh River and is the easternmost extension of a relatively undeveloped landscape stretching from the wooded slopes east of Steel City to west Easton. The ten-mile section of forested islands, floodplains, and upland slopes provides habitat for many birds and mammals.

Oak and hickory dominate the upland forested slopes while the bottomland forest consists mainly of American Sycamore, Cottonwood, Box Elder, Silver Maple, and Black Walnut. The understory contains many species of brushy vegetation and wildflowers. A two-mile section of the canal was rewatered in 1975 and is used for mule-drawn canal boat rides. Within the park lie several islands in the Lehigh River. Island Park is the largest of these, covering approximately 100 acres. It is the most ecologically significant, with a 5- to 10-acre emergent marsh wetland running through it.

Land for this park was purchased in 1962 by Hugh Moore, best remembered for his invention of the Dixie cup. Mr. Moore donated the land to the city of Easton for conservation and passive recreation.

Birds. The river attracts many species of waterfowl and other water-loving birds. Common and Hooded Mergansers, Bufflehead, Common Goldeneye, and Green-winged Teal are seen in migration. Wood Ducks nest on the islands. Large numbers of gulls, sometimes including Bonaparte's and Great Black-backed, winter on the river, with Glaucous, Iceland, and Lesser Black-backed Gulls as rare visitors. The Chain Dam is where the greatest gull concentrations occur. Common Loons, Bald Eagles, Osprey, and Peregrine Falcons have also passed through. Pied-billed Grebes, Great Egrets, and Great Blue and Green Herons are present in the summer. Black-crowned Night-Herons occasionally appear in late summer.

Large numbers of songbirds nest in or pass through the wooded banks of the river, including a number of species not easily found elsewhere in the Valley. Veerys, Orchard Orioles, Rose-breasted Grosbeaks, Yellow-throated Vireos, and Great Crested Flycatchers are among the park breeders. Many warblers nest here, including a high density of American Redstarts, along with Northern Parula, Blue-winged, and Worm-eating Warblers. Yellow-throated Warblers, a rare breeder for the Lehigh Valley, can be found here. Cerulean and Prothonotary Warblers are occasionally seen. Swallows are common over the river. The trail heading east in the northern portion of the park beginning at Hope Rd. provides excellent birding for these species.

Directions. To reach the eastern and southern parts of the park: From the intersection of Rt. 22 with Rt. 512, take Rt. 22 7.0 mi. east to the 25th St. exit in Easton. At the end of the exit ramp, bear right onto 25th St. and follow it 1.5 mi. south. Just before the Glendon Bridge, turn right onto Lehigh Dr. Go 0.5 mi. to the stop sign and turn right, then cross over the entrance bridge into the park. At the end of the bridge, turn right again and proceed 0.5 mi. to the main parking lot.

To reach Hope Rd. and the trail heading east through the northern portion of the park: From the intersection of Rt. 22 with Rt. 191 (Linden St.), take Rt. 191 south about 0.7 mi. to Oakland Rd. Turn left onto Oakland Rd. and follow it 1.8 mi. to Easton Ave. (William Penn Hwy.). Turn left onto Easton Ave. and go 0.3 mi. to the intersection with Farmersville Rd. Turn right onto Farmersville Rd. and follow it 1.3 mi. to Freemansburg Ave. Turn left and take Freemansburg Ave. 1.3 mi. to Hope Rd. There is no street sign as of this writing; Hope Rd. is the first right after the traffic lights at the intersection with Rt. 33. Turn right onto Hope Rd. and follow it about 1.0 mi. to its end at the Bethlehem Boat Club entrance. Do not park on or enter boat club property. There is a small parking area to the left at the head of the trail into Hugh Moore Park.

The trail along the river can also be accessed by taking Farmersville Rd. all the way down to the river. Heading east from here on the trail for about 1 mi. will bring you to the Hope Rd./ Bethlehem Boat Club area. Alternatively, continue on Freemansburg Ave. about 1.0 mi. past Hope Rd. to Stone's Crossing Rd. and take Stone's Crossing down to the river and trails. (Stone's Crossing becomes one-way in the other direction as you approach the river; park and walk the rest of the way down.)

To access the northern portion of the park farther east, including the Chain Dam, enter from Riverview Park in Palmer. For directions, see the Riverview Park site description.

Notes. (1) Black Bear, Bobcat, and River Otter have been observed within the park. (2) This corridor is under increasing pressure from highway projects, commercial development, and a new public boat launch. Public efforts may be needed to preserve its viability as wildlife habitat. (3) An outhouse is open year round at the main parking lot. (4) The park is of considerable historic interest. Canal structures, locks, 19th-century industrial ruins, and a locktender's house museum are contained within it. Canal boat rides are available in the warm weather. (Use the eastern entrance for these areas). A canal museum is nearby. For further information, contact Hugh Moore Historical Park & Museums at (610) 559-6613 or check their web site, <www.canals.org/hmpark.htm>. (5) It is not yet clear if the Rt. 33 bridge recently built over the river at Hope Rd. will impact the birdlife in that area.

21. Riverview Park

Description. Located off of South 25th St. below Easton, Palmer's Riverview Park abuts the Lehigh River and provides varied habitat including fields, riparian woodland, and the river itself. It sits within a larger area of preserved land that constitutes the northern portion of Hugh Moore Park. A walking trail follows the river, connecting to the trail through Hugh Moore Park. A wider trail along an old railroad bed is accessible from above the baseball field.

Birds. A visit at any time of year can be productive. In the spring, the sycamores and other trees lining the river's shores attract woodland birds including Pileated Woodpeckers, Eastern Wood-Pewees, Wood Thrushes, and Ovenbirds, along with many of the more common species. The open grassy areas surrounding the parking lot and baseball fields are good for Eastern Bluebirds. The river itself can be productive for waterfowl and gulls during the fall and winter.

The Chain Dam, part of Hugh Moore Park, is most easily accessed by parking at Riverview Park and walking the river trail upriver about a quarter mile. This area is especially productive for wintering gulls (see the Hugh Moore Park site description).

Directions. From the intersection of Rt. 22 with Rt. 512, take Rt. 22 east 7.0 mi. to the 25th St. exit in Easton. At the end of the exit ramp, bear right onto 25th St. and follow it 1.5 mi. south. Just before the Glendon Bridge, turn right onto Lehigh Dr. Almost immediately (about 100 yds.), turn right into the park.

Note. The park is open dawn to dusk all year but may be inaccessible when the river runs high.

22. Green Pond

Description. Green Pond is a small, undeveloped pond in a lightly developed area. Several farm fields nearby flood regularly in the spring, and there are brushy areas around the edges of the fields and pond.

Birds. The pond itself attracts ducks and geese and an occasional grebe or egret, mainly in the spring. The flooded fields are the more significant feature of this area and attract migrating shorebirds and ducks, primarily in April and May. In recent years, large numbers of Snow Geese have also stopped here. Brushy areas around the pond and fields hold sparrows and other songbirds, and swallows and hawks are seen in the vicinity.

Directions. From the intersection of Rt. 22 with Rt. 191, head south on Rt. 191 (Linden St.) for 0.8 mi. to Oakland Rd. Turn left and follow Oakland Rd. 0.8 mi. Turn left at the stop sign onto Hecktown Rd. and follow Hecktown Rd. 0.6 mi. Turn right onto Green Pond Rd. and go 1.2 mi. At the T intersection, turn left; Green Pond is just ahead on the left. There is a small paved parking area just off the road near the pond. The fields are around the bend in the road. There is no shoulder on either side of the road, so either park at the pond and walk to the fields, or pull over well past the bend in the road and keep an eye out for approaching traffic.

Note. The farm fields are under threat of development but no specific plan has been adopted as of this writing.

23. State Game Lands #205

Description. State Game Lands #205 in Lowhill Township is a 1506-acre area managed for deer and other game animals. It contains a mixture of open fields, brushy tangles, and coniferous and deciduous woodlands. The area is generally hilly. A section of the Jordan Creek is within its boundaries. There are several dirt roads that provide easy access to most of the area. Birding is generally done by walking or driving the dirt roads.

Birds. The area is best in migration, although it is also worth visiting at other seasons. The wooded stream valley areas have some of the best birding. Although one of the largest natural areas left in the Lehigh Valley, it has not been birded regularly, so surprises are possible. Look for woodland birds such as thrushes, vireos, and warblers in migration, and look for sparrows in grassy and brushy sections.

Directions. From the intersection of Rt. 22 with Rt. 100, go north on Rt. 100 5.6 mi. (continuing past a sign labeled "Game Preserve" at Kistler Rd.) and turn right onto Game Preserve Rd. Game Preserve Rd. is a well-maintained dirt road that goes down a long hill. The game lands are on the left stretching slightly more than a mile. Adjoining private lands may also provide good birding if they are not posted. At 0.5 mi. on Game Preserve Rd., there is a small parking area on the left (just beyond a gated area with a "No Parking" sign). You can walk down the dirt road beyond the gate to the Jordan Creek. A second parking area is another 0.2 mi. farther on Game Preserve Rd.

In the past, access to other parts of the game lands has been possible by following Game Preserve Rd. 1.9 mi. to the intersection of Game Preserve Rd. and Kistler Rt., turning left onto Kistler Rd., and then following this road across the creek and back into the game lands. At this writing, the bridge over the creek has been taken out of service. Other parts of the game lands can be accessed only by returning to Rt. 100 and working your way in from roads farther north, or by following Game Preserve Rd. past Kistler Rd. several miles to its entry to the Trexler Game Preserve and connecting roads that run back into the game lands.

Notes. (1) Since this is a hunting area, it is best to visit on Sundays when most hunting is prohibited, and to avoid it completely during the fall hunting season. **(2)** The nearby Trexler Game Preserve is also worth a visit. **(3)** Watch for traffic if birding the roadsides on foot.

24. Whitehall Parkway and Ironton Rail Trail/ D & L Trail

Description. Whitehall Parkway, a Whitehall Township park, is largely wooded with the Coplay Creek running through it. The grounds include an abandoned cement company with many deteriorating stone buildings, a water-filled quarry, a dry quarry, mounds of stone tailings, and open fields. Several of the field areas are managed for wildlife. Vegetation has developed mostly in the last 50 years. Mixed deciduous woods, Red-cedar stands, and many berrying plants and assorted weed growth are present, along with a very few old growth deciduous trees and conifers.

The Ironton Rail Trail is a converted railroad bed that passes through the Whitehall Parkway and continues east and west for about 7 miles. From the Whitehall Parkway heading west, the trail passes through wooded areas and brushy fields along the Coplay Creek for about 1.5 mi. This section can provide good birding. Much of the trail east of Rt. 145 passes developed areas. However, from its easternmost edge one can head north up the D & L (Delaware & Lehigh) Trail, overlooking the Lehigh River on the right with deciduous woods and brushy areas to the left. The approximately 2.5 mile stretch up to Laury's Station moves progressively farther from development.

Birds. Winter residents of the Parkway include Brown Creeper, Winter Wren, Cedar Waxwings, and kinglets. Spring and fall migration are good for warblers, vireos, and other songbirds. Indigo Bunting, Baltimore and Orchard Oriole, Scarlet Tanager, and Yellow-billed Cuckoo are among the nesting species. Raptors including American Kestrels and Cooper's Hawks can be seen year round.

Records are not available for the rail trails, but a short winter walk on the D & L trail produced Bufflehead, Common Merganser, and Herring Gull on the river, as well as common waterfowl, Ring-billed Gulls, and wintering songbirds. This area deserves more exploration.

Directions. To reach the Parkway, from the intersection of Rt. 22 with Rt. 145 (MacArthur Rd.) in Whitehall, take Rt. 145 north for 3.7 mi. to Chestnut St. Turn left onto Chestnut to the

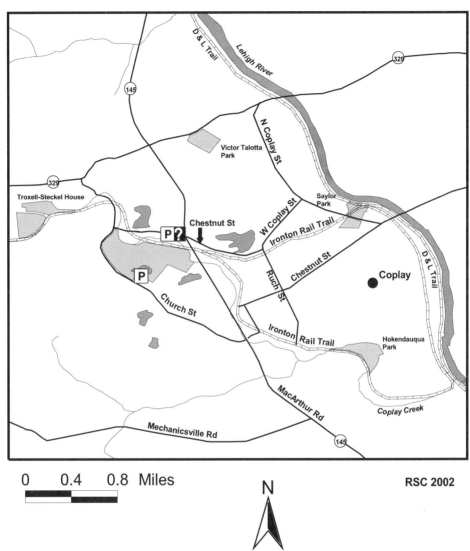

0   0.4   0.8 Miles   N   RSC 2002

parking area 0.2 mi. on the left. (A larger, paved parking lot is also available 0.7 mi. farther by continuing on Chestnut to the intersection with S. Church Rd. and following S. Church to the left.)

The western portion of the Ironton Rail Trail can be accessed just below the Chestnut St. parking lot at the Parkway. To reach its eastern edge and the connection to the D & L trail, from the Parkway lot, turn right onto Chestnut St. Follow Chestnut St. (crossing MacArthur Rd.) for 0.7 mi. Bear left onto W. Coplay Rd. Follow W. Coplay 0.5 mi. and turn right onto N. Coplay Rd. In 0.3 mi., turn left into the Saylor Park parking lot. Follow the Ironton Rail Trail past the cement kilns toward the river, and head north (left) onto the D & L Trail.

Notes. (1) Parkway trail maps are available in the parking lot on Chestnut St. **(2)** A portable toilet is located near each parking lot in the Parkway.

25. Jordan Creek Parkway

Description. Jordan Creek Parkway is a 296-acre Lehigh County park that surrounds the Jordan Creek just north of Allentown. In addition to the creek, habitats include two ponds, old-growth woods, relatively new woods, and low-growth fields. Trails both wide and narrow wind throughout the park.

Birds. Many species of vireos, thrushes, warblers, and other songbirds along with woodpeckers and flycatchers nest in or migrate through these woods. Occasional shorebirds (Solitary and Spotted Sandpiper) and both Green and Great Blue Herons can be found along the creek. Great Horned Owls nest in these woods, and Cooper's Hawk has nested in the past. Several other species of raptors migrate through the park.

The following provides a walking tour beginning from the main parking lot near the tennis courts. To reach this lot, see **Directions**.

From the parking lot, before going over the bridges, scan the grassy fields to the left for various sparrows. Near the first bridge, Warbling Vireos can be found nesting in the trees along the creek between the tennis courts and the bridge. In the spring, also keep an eye out here for Baltimore and Orchard Orioles and American Redstarts.

After the second bridge, the main path continues straight with a smaller trail to the right that follows the creek. In winter, the main path is the choice to take. Watch for White-throated Sparrows, Dark-eyed Juncos, Brown Creeper, White-breasted Nuthatches, woodpeckers, and other woodland birds. The creekside trail is a bit longer but good during spring migration for warblers, vireos, Rose-breasted Grosbeak, Scarlet Tanager, and other songbirds.

The main path intersects with a pipeline. At that intersection during migration scan the tall trees for warblers, vireos, Scarlet Tanagers, and Baltimore Orioles. Take a right turn along the pipeline and walk down to the creek to the creekside trail. Turn left at the creek to continue on the creekside trail. This trail eventually returns to the main path that goes through the entire park. At this point either:

(a) take a right on the main path, which intersects with another concrete bridge where Eastern Phoebes nest. Continuing over this bridge will take you into a pleasant older section of woods. Saw-whet Owl has been found there in winter. Backtrack to the main path to exit this area.

(b) take a left onto the main path, heading back toward the parking lot. You will come upon a lean-to storage building. This area is usually good for Eastern Towhees, Scarlet Tanager, and sparrows. Continue on the main path. Just past the lean-to buildings, a right turn leads into a small clearing. Again, there are two choices:

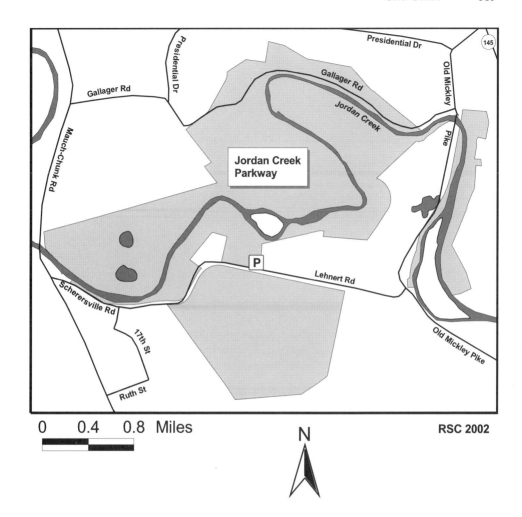

0   0.4   0.8   Miles   N   **RSC 2002**

(a) If you take the right turn into the clearing, a path leads into the woods to the left. After the woods, you will come out at the pipeline. Turning left onto the pipeline takes you back to the main path of the park.

(b) For a shorter walk, instead of turning right into the small clearing, continue on the main path to intersect with the pipeline.

Either route is good for Wood Thrush, Great Crested and other flycatchers, Veerys, and Hermit Thrushes in the appropriate season.

To extend your walk, after either of the above two choices, take a right turn at the pipeline and follow it down the big hill into the fields, which are good for sparrows, gnatcatchers, warblers, etc. Willow Flycatcher has been found here. Walk around the fields to two ponds, watching for Wood Ducks that nest on the ponds. You will end up on the footbridge that goes over the creek into the public gardens. Over the bridge, walk along the creek to the left. Watch the banks for four species of swallows, Swainson's Thrush, and Green Heron. Continue on this path along the creek, (passing the only nearby house). When the path bears to the right, you will come out into the grassy fields and main entrance to the park.

Directions. From the intersection of Rt. 22 with 15th St. in Allentown, take the 15th St. exit and head north (right) at the end of the exit ramp onto Mauch Chunk Rd. Follow Mauch Chunk Rd. 0.7 mi. and make a sharp right at the light onto Scherersville Rd. Follow Scherersville Rd. 0.5 mi. to the main parking lot just past the tennis courts and maintenance buildings.

Notes. (1) Restrooms are located next to the tennis courts but are only open in spring and summer. **(2)** In mid-day and early evening, the park receives fairly heavy general use.

26. Fogelsville Quarry and Dam

Description. The Fogelsville Quarry is a former stone quarry now filled with water. It sits at the edge of the Upper Macungie Township Park, which contains mowed playing fields, a picnic area, and a small deciduous woodlot. Just down the road, an undeveloped area south of a dam provides a small wetland and pond adjacent to a wooded slope. The wet area can be scouted from the roadside, and a trail runs from a side road along the hillside.

Birds. The quarry attracts a good variety of waterbirds including Common Loons, Pied-billed Grebes, Double-crested Cormorants, geese, American Coots, and many species of diving and puddle ducks, along with Great Blue Herons at the edge. At least two Great Blue Heron nests have been present in recent years, with activity most visible in April. Another recent feature has been large numbers of Snow Geese passing through in March, with an occasional Ross's Goose or White-fronted Goose among them. Birding is generally best in the late fall and early spring, though the Christmas Bird Count often finds some interesting waterfowl present.

The wet area north of the quarry and its surrounding brushy areas, along with the hillside behind it, are home to various woodpeckers and songbirds. Swamp Sparrows can often be found in the winter. Nesting species include Wood Ducks on the dam pond and Orchard Orioles on the opposite side of the road. Migrants occasionally seen here are Great Egret, Hooded Merganser, Osprey, Spotted Sandpiper, and, rarely, Black-crowned Night-Heron. Great Blue Herons are often present very early in the morning, and Great Horned Owls and Eastern Screech-Owls can sometimes be heard in the early spring at dusk or dawn.

Directions. From the intersection of Rt. 22 with Rt. 100 in Fogelsville, take Rt. 100 north 1.0 mi. to Haasadahl Rd. Turn right onto Haasadahl and then immediately turn right again into a small parking lot. The quarry is behind the fence to the right of the parking lot. To get to the dam area, follow Haasadahl Rd. north 0.5 mi., just past the intersection with Hilltop Rd. There is a small turnout on the left side of the road that can be used for parking, and another one 0.1 mi. farther. The hillside trail is accessed from Hilltop Rd.

Notes. (1) A scope is needed to identify most birds at the quarry. (2) Traffic is sparse but fast-moving in the dam area, so be sure to stand off of the road. (3) There are restrooms in the park building near the quarry lot, but they may not be open in all seasons. Other bathrooms can be found at fast food restaurants on Rt. 100.

27. Trexler Park

Description. This 134-acre Allentown city park has open grassy areas, mixed deciduous and coniferous wooded patches, and a shallow four-acre lake. Cedar Creek flows through the park. Although much of the space between clusters of trees is lawn, parts of the park are increasingly managed for wildlife. An area along a portion of the creek has been planted with shrubs and high grass to attract wildlife, and underbrush has been allowed to grow up within stands of trees. The park contains a 1.2 mile long macadam path that is used extensively by bikers, joggers and walkers. The path provides convenient and easy access to most areas of the park. A high level of public use limits bird watching opportunities during midday.

Birds. The lake attracts common waterfowl all year and an occasional migrant in spring and fall, particularly when fewer people are present. A Belted Kingfisher is frequently seen. The wooded areas attract migrating warblers, vireos, and other songbirds, particularly in spring, and woodland birds all year. The base of the brushy/wooded hill and the top of this hill tend to be the best spots.

Directions. From the intersection of Rt. 22 with Cedar Crest Blvd. (Rt. 29), take Cedar Crest Blvd. south 1.5 mi. to Broadway. Turn right onto Broadway and go 0.1 mi. to Springhouse Road. Turn right onto Springhouse Rd. and continue 0.2 mi. to the parking lot entrance on right.

Notes. (1) The macadam path through the park is wheelchair-accessible from the parking lot. (2) A handicapped-accessible restroom is located near the path opposite the lake.

28. Cedar Creek Park and Lake Muhlenberg

Description. This long, narrow Allentown city park is a watershed area of Cedar Creek. In addition to the creek, included within park bounds are Cedar Beach (a public swimming area), the Allentown Rose Garden, and Lake Muhlenberg, a shallow 6-acre impoundment of the creek. The park receives extensive public use. A recently introduced paddle-boat concession at the lake limits bird watching during the summer.

Birds. Over the years, many migrating waterfowl species have been seen at Lake Muhlenberg. Increased public use and removal of vegetation around the pond have greatly reduced migratory sightings in recent years. Common waterfowl species are present all year. Songbirds may be seen throughout the park, especially during migration.

Directions. From the intersection of Rt. 22 with Cedar Crest Blvd. (Rt. 29) in Allentown, take Cedar Crest Blvd. south 1.5 mi. to the intersection with Parkway Blvd. Turn left onto Parkway Blvd. The park is on the right. Go approx. 1.0 mi., crossing Ott St., to reach Lake Muhlenberg. Cars can be parked along Parkway Blvd.

Note. A handicapped-accessible restroom is available at Honochick Dr. on the south edge of the park, west of Ott St.

29. Little Lehigh Park (Lehigh Parkway)

Description. The Little Lehigh Park is a 575-acre stream valley park that generally follows the Little Lehigh Creek in Allentown. The area along the creek is mostly grass but is marshy in spots. The hillsides that border the park are wooded and brushy. In early morning, the sun gives excellent lighting to the wooded hillside on the west side of the stream.

Birds. The park is best in migration, although it is also worth visiting during other seasons. The best birding is generally on the wooded hillsides that are easily accessible from gravel pedestrian paths running on both sides of the creek through most of the park. There are also several dirt paths that go through the woods.

Particularly good spots include the hillside on the northwestern-most edge of the park around the bend in the stream, the area near Bogert's Bridge (an old covered bridge) just north of Oxford Dr., and the wooded hillside just north of where Fish Hatchery Rd. crosses through the park. A short walk upstream from Bogert's Bridge brings you to an area of pine trees that attracts White-breasted and Red-breasted Nuthatches, Ruby-crowned and Golden-crowned Kinglets, and Yellow-rumped Warblers in the winter, and Cape May and Pine Warblers in migration. The old willow trees that border much of the stream also attract many birds, particularly fall warblers.

Several seasonally marshy areas along the stream attract Swamp Sparrows during migration. The wooded hillsides are best for woodpeckers, flycatchers, kinglets, vireos, warblers, and other edge-loving birds.

Directions. From the intersection of I-78 with Cedar Crest Blvd. (Rt. 29), take Cedar Crest Blvd. south 0.4 mi. and turn left at the light onto Fish Hatchery Rd. Follow Fish Hatchery Rd. 1.1 mi. to its end and turn left at the light onto Oxford Dr. In 0.2 mi., take the first right onto Park Dr. (There is no street sign for Park Dr.) There is a parking lot 0.5 north on Park Dr. (Another lot is 0.3 mi. farther, across a bridge that crosses the creek, and third lot is an additional 0.7 mi. north. However, as of this writing, the bridge is closed to traffic, and these lots can only be accessed by entering the park from its north end, off Jefferson St. in Allentown.)

Notes. (1) An outhouse, open in warm weather, is located near Bogert's Bridge. (2) The east side of the park can also be accessed by walking across Bogert's Bridge. (3) The level gravel paths provide easy walking.

30. Bob Rodale Cycling and Fitness Park

Description. The Bob Rodale Cycling and Fitness Park, owned by Lehigh County, is known to local birders by its former name, the Trexlertown Pines. The northeast portion of the park consists of mowed grassy expanses dotted with trees, shrubs, and flowering plants. The remainder of the park is a 45-acre dense forest patch. Much of the patch is coniferous, though some sections are becoming increasingly deciduous. Several low-lying areas remain wet most years, and a trickle of water runs through the southeast end. A creek just outside the park boundaries also provides a water source. A paved path for bicycling/rollerblading runs through the park, including the woodlot, and receives substantial use, but foot trails through the trees are quiet and little used.

Birds. The open grassy areas attract various songbirds including Northern Mockingbirds, and nest boxes house Tree Swallows and House Wrens during the breeding season. Eastern Bluebirds have also been seen and may nest here. The wooded patch holds a variety of songbirds including many Wood Thrushes in spring and summer. During the summer, Indigo Buntings can be found along the edge where the cycling path cuts through the woods. Both Great Horned Owl and Cooper's Hawk have been known to nest in the trees. Red-breasted Nuthatches have been present in both winter and summer. In irruption years, the winter numbers can be high. The wet area at the southeast end of the park attracts Red-winged Blackbirds in migration.

Fields just south of Rt. 222 in this vicinity are also worth scouting for birds, primarily Horned Larks and Snow Buntings in the winter, and Vesper and Savannah Sparrows in the spring and summer.

Directions. From the intersection of Rt. 22 with Rt. 100 in Fogelsville, take Rt. 100 south for about 2.8 mi. to the intersection with Rt. 222 (Hamilton Blvd.). Turn right onto Rt. 222 and go 0.3 mi. to Mosser Rd. Bear right onto Mosser Rd. The parking lot is a short distance up on the left, across from the entrance to the Lehigh Valley Velodrome.

Notes. (1) Red squirrels are common in the coniferous trees. **(2)** A portable toilet is located in the parking lot. Other bathrooms are available at gas stations and fast food restaurants on Rt. 222 within a mile east of the park. **(3)** Watch out for poison ivy near the trails.

31. Rodale Experimental Farm

Description. The Rodale Experimental Farm in Maxatawny provides a unique birding site as a working farm open to the public. Birders can explore habitats normally requiring permission from the landowner. The area includes fields, hedge rows, orchard, small ponds and streams, and a wooded area. Bluebird houses are maintained throughout the property. All farming is organic.

Birds. The habitat diversity and organic methods make this area a good site for many northeastern species. One of the best areas is along the brushy margins of the stream that goes west of the farm. Waterproof boots are needed for walking here. White-crowned Sparrows are regular in this area in the winter.

Fields just south of Rt. 222 in the vicinity of the farm are also worth scouting for raptors and grassland birds.

Directions. From the intersection of Rt. 22 with Rt. 100 in Fogelsville, take Rt. 100 south for about 2.8 mi. to the intersection with Rt. 222 (Hamilton Blvd.). Turn right onto 222 and follow it about 5 mi. south. Just after passing through the small town of Maxatawny, turn right onto Grim Rd. (Look for a sign for the Rodale Institute on the right.) Follow Grim Rd. 0.9 mi. to the stop sign at Siegfriedale Road. Turn left and go 0.5 mi. to the parking lot on the left. Parking is also available at barns farther down on the right.

Notes. (1) A map and brochures are available in the bookstore, which is open 9:00 a.m. to 5:00 p.m., Mon. through Sat. all year and Sunday afternoons during the summer. A donation of $3 is requested for the map. The Institute can be reached at (610) 683-1400; the bookstore number is (610) 683-6009. Birders are allowed to walk the property outside of operating hours. **(2)** Restrooms near the bookstore are open when the bookstore is. Other restrooms are available at gas and fast food shops along Rt. 222.

32. Smith Lane and Dorney Landfill

Description. The Smith Lane area near Alburtis is a series of open farm fields. Unpaved but well-maintained roads provide good access. The Dorney landfill area nearby consists of a shallow retaining pond and surrounding grassy fields.

Birds. The Smith Lane area is the best remaining spot in Lehigh County for winter field birds including Horned Larks, Snow Buntings, and occasional Lapland Longspurs. The optimal time to look for them is when manure is spread on top of the snow. The undigested seeds in the manure form a huge ground-level feeder for the birds. In good years, several thousand birds can be seen wheeling and turning across the fields. When there is no snow, there may still be birds, but they are almost impossible to see on the ground. Wait for them to fly, then note where they land and scan that area. Savannah Sparrows are also regular here in winter. Summer birds include Horned Larks and sometimes Grasshopper Sparrows.

The Dorney landfill area is also productive for grassland species. In winter, the fields surrounding the landfill may contain Horned Larks, Snow Buntings, Lapland Longspurs, and Savannah Sparrows. In summer, Eastern Meadowlarks and Grasshopper, Vesper, and Savannah Sparrows have been present and may even breed in the area. During migration, American Pipits and Bobolinks may be present. In rainy weather, the farm fields flood and provide good shorebird habitat.

The landfill itself contains a small pond that can be viewed by standing on the mound near the entrance gate. Shorebirds can be present at the muddy edge any time between mid-March and November, with the best times being mid-April through May and mid-July through mid-September. The best time to check is during or immediately after fronts that produce periods of prolonged rain, when less common species may be grounded during their migration.

This area can also be good for waterfowl at almost any time of year. From mid-February to early April, thousands of Canada and Snow Geese may be present. These flocks should be checked for the occasional rarity; both Ross's and Greater White-fronted Geese have been seen here. If no geese are present in this time period, try the nearby Fogelsville Quarry (see the Fogelsville Dam and Quarry site description), where many of the geese that visit this area go to roost. Ruddy Ducks and Green-winged Teal have been seen in summer.

Directions. To reach Smith Lane, from the intersection of Rt. 22 with Rt. 100 in Fogelsville, take Rt. 100 south about 2.8 mi. to the intersection with Rt. 222 (Hamilton Blvd.). From this point, continue south on Rt. 100 for 1.0 mi. to the traffic light at Spring Creek Rd. Turn right and follow this road for 1.8 mi. into Alburtis. Immediately after crossing the railroad tracks, turn right onto Front St. Continue 0.6 mi. on Front St. (which becomes Longswamp Rd.) and turn right onto Smith Lane. The best birding areas are on Smith Lane for about a mile starting at the first intersection with an unmarked gravel road on the right (at 0.5 mi.), and down the gravel road for about a mile.

To reach the Dorney landfill area from Smith Lane, continue north on Smith Lane until it ends at Mertztown Rd (which may not be labeled). Turn left and follow Mertztown Rd. At 0.8 mi., just past a 25 mph bend and several farm buildings, Mertztown Rd. leaves the main road and makes a sharp turn to the right at an unmarked intersection. Take this right and continue on Mertztown Rd. for 1.2 mi. Turn right onto Mertz Rd. and follow it 0.7 mi. to a T intersection with Dorney Rd. Turn right and go 0.3 mi. on Dorney Rd. Park near the gate to the fence that surrounds the landfill.

Notes. (1) Traffic is light in the Smith Rd. vicinity, but pull off to the side as much as possible. **(2)** The best winter viewing is from inside the car. It acts as a blind and also protects you from the cold wind that can sweep across the fields. A scope may be needed, but often the birds will come out onto the road looking for grit.

33. Kalmbach Memorial Park

Description. Kalmbach Memorial Park in Macungie is a 20-acre tract of varied habitats, including a stand of conifers, a stream, meadows, deciduous woods, and butterfly gardens. There are easy loop trails, a bird blind with several feeders, birdhouses, two bridges, and several benches.

Birds. This area is very good in spring and fall migration for songbirds. Winter birds include Red-breasted Nuthatches, Yellow-rumped Warblers, Yellow-bellied Sapsuckers, and Golden-crowned Kinglets. A Pine Warbler stayed for the 2000 Christmas Bird Count week.

Directions. From the intersection of Rt. 22 with Rt. 100 in Fogelsville, take Rt. 100 south for about 2.8 mi. to the intersection with Rt. 222 (Hamilton Blvd.). From this point, continue south on Rt. 100 another 3.9 mi. into Macungie. After crossing the railroad tracks, go 0.5 mi. and turn right onto Chestnut St. Turn right again at the first street by the stand of conifers (Cotton St.). The park will be on the left. The entrance to a good-sized parking lot is on the left, just past the house and barn. Turn right into the parking lot.

Notes. (1) The park is open from dawn to dusk. (2) An excellent trail map noting the various habitats is on the board at the edge of the parking lot. (3) Bathrooms are available in the lower level of the barn when it is open unless there is a paid program in progress.

34. Pool Wildlife Sanctuary

Description. The Pool Wildlife Sanctuary, owned by the Wildlands Conservancy, is located near Emmaus. The 72-acre property includes a stream (the Little Lehigh Creek), man-made ponds, deciduous woods, fields, and shrubby, and brushy areas. A trail system winds through the sanctuary. The Conservancy maintains bluebird boxes, feeders, and a bird blind.

Birds. Resident species include Wild Turkey, Cooper's Hawk, Red-tailed Hawk, Great Horned Owl, and Belted Kingfisher. Great Blue Herons are generally present and have been seen roosting along the stream in winter. Migrant warblers and other songbirds can be found in season. An occasional Spotted Sandpiper has been present along the stream. Indigo Buntings nest near the bee hives on the Pheasant Run trail.

Directions. From the intersection of I-78 with Cedar Crest Blvd. (Rt. 29), go south on Cedar Crest Blvd. 1.5 mi. to the stoplight at Riverbend Rd. (Look for a sign for the sanctuary on the southeast corner). Turn left onto Riverbend and follow it 0.8 mi. to Orchid Pl. Turn right onto Orchid Pl. and follow it 0.3 mi. downhill to the sanctuary entrance on the right. Parking is to the left of the barn.

Notes. (1) Maps are available at the information board. A birdlist is available in the office, which is open 8:00 a.m. to 4:00 p.m. weekdays. The environmental education center is open Sunday afternoons (2:00 to 4:00 p.m.). (2) The Conservancy conducts nature programs. For information, call the office at (610) 965-4397. (3) An outhouse near the education building and a portable toilet near the pavilion are open at all times.

35. Reimert Memorial Bird Haven

Description. The Reimert Memorial Bird Haven in Macungie is owned and maintained by the Wildlands Conservancy. It is an 11-acre tract of deciduous wooded hillside. There is a loop trail through the property beginning at the far end of the parking lot and proceeding uphill.

Birds. This area is good for many woodland species, especially in migration. Hooded and Kentucky Warblers have nested here.

Directions. From the intersection of Rt. 22 with Rt.100 in Fogelsville, take Rt. 100 south for about 2.8 mi. to the intersection with Rt. 222 (Hamilton Blvd.). From this point, continue south on Rt. 100 another 3.9 mi. into Macungie. After crossing the railroad tracks, take the third right onto Church St. (As of this writing, the street sign is missing; Church follows Pine.) Church will become Mountain Rd. Follow Church/Mountain Rd. 1.0 mi. to the sanctuary entrance on the left. A blind curve makes left turns tricky; you may prefer to pass the property and turn around to enter. There is parking for one or two cars outside the gate.

Note. If more than one or two cars will be present, call the Pool Wildlife Sanctuary at (610) 965-4397 and obtain a key for the gate to access the parking lot.

36. Green Lane Park and Upper Perkiomen Valley Park

Description. Green Lane Park (formerly Green Lane Reservoir) and Upper Perkiomen Valley Park encompass nearly 3,000 acres of open space in western Montgomery County. An 800-acre lake, two smaller lakes, and a variety of terrestrial habitats make the area attractive to a wide variety of birds. Terrestrial habitats include oak and mixed forest, conifer plantations, Red-cedar barrens, fallow fields, and a shallow marsh/meadow.

Birds. The Green Lane Park/Upper Perkiomen Valley Park checklist includes over 250 species, but waterbirds are the main attraction. Thirty-three species of ducks and geese have been recorded, including Barnacle, Ross's, and Greater White-fronted Goose, Brant, Long-tailed Duck (Oldsquaw), and all three scoter species. Diving birds, including loons, grebes, and cormorants, are most easily found at the Walt Rd. boat launch area, especially after rainstorms in March to April and October to November. Early morning is best at this site, as heavy boat traffic usually spooks the birds. Dabbling ducks can best be seen at Church Rd. (where the best light is after 2:00 p.m.) and Knight Lake. Wood Ducks breed at Knight Lake and a good variety of other species are often present in migration.

Green Lane is also well-known for its shorebirds during fall migration. Extensive mudflats in the area of Church Rd. are present most years and have attracted over 30 species of shorebirds. Fall migration begins by mid-July and continues into November if the water level is low. Among the shorebirds seen here have been Black-bellied and American Golden-Plover, American Avocet, Ruddy Turnstone, White-rumped, Baird's, Stilt, and Buff-breasted Sandpipers, Sanderling, all three phalaropes, and Hudsonian Godwit. Most of these birds are rare and not to be expected every year.

Herons, gulls, and terns can also be found at Church Rd. in the appropriate seasons. Field birds such as American Pipit and Snow Bunting can sometimes be found on the mudflats in late autumn. American Bittern, Sora and Virginia Rail are all considered rare in the marshy area here. Sparrows including White-crowned, Swamp, Savannah, and Lincoln's can be found in the marsh most years.

Green Lane has many other productive birding habitats as well. The tall-grass agricultural lease fields along Church and Knight Rds. often host raptors including Northern Harriers,

Rough-legged Hawks, and Short-eared Owls. Check the fields along Church Rd. just before dusk from December to March for the owls. Up to 7 birds have been seen here, though 1 or 2 is more likely, and in some years there are none. These same fields produce Eastern Meadowlark and a variety of sparrows year-round. Hock Rd. opposite the Church Rd. parking lot can also produce raptors, and, in early spring, American Woodcock.

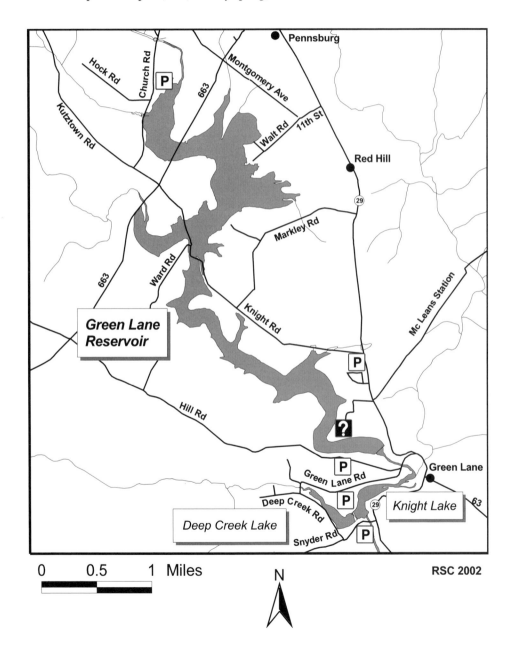

RSC 2002

Woodland birding for warblers and other migrants can also be good in the park, including on the trails at the park office on Hill Rd. or behind the Nature Center. The Nature Center has a feeding station and observation room which are operational September to May. In addition to the usual feeder species, Brown Creeper, Purple Finch, and Fox Sparrow can be found here most winters. Pine Siskins are sometimes present.

Directions. To begin at the Nature Center, from the intersection of I-78 with Rt. 29 (Cedar Crest Blvd.) in Allentown, take Rt. 29 south for 14.7 mi. to the intersection with Rt. 663. (Rt. 29 makes a sharp right in Emmaus and a sharp left at the traffic light in the village of Hereford where it splits from Rt. 100; follow the signs.) From the intersection with Rt. 663, continue 3.7 mi. farther on Rt. 29 and turn right into the Nature Center drive. (The sign is easy to miss; look for the Marlborough Elementary School at the same spot). Follow the driveway to the first building on the right.

To go directly to the Church Rd. shorebird spot, take Rt. 29 south as above to where Rt. 29 makes a sharp left and splits from Rt. 100 at Hereford. From this point, continue on Rt. 29 2.9 mi. and turn right at the traffic light onto Water St. just before a railroad overpass. Take Water St., which turns into Church Rd., 2.7 mi. The parking area will be on the left.

Notes. (**1**) Maps, a bird list, and a sightings log are available at the Nature Center. Restrooms are available at the Nature Center, Walt Rd. boat launch area, and the park office on Hill Rd. (**2**) Church Rd. has a sightings log sheet, maps, and checklists, but no restrooms. (**3**) The lake can be very crowded with boats and fishermen, especially between April and October. Boating and fishing are prohibited at Church Rd. and behind the Nature Center. Horses are permitted on all park trails except the Hemlock Point Trail at the Nature Center. (**4**) Park hours are 6:00 a.m. to sunset year-round. (**5**) The site has been designated as an Important Bird Area (IBA) by Pennsylvania Audubon Society.

37. Oberly Road (Alpha, New Jersey)

Description. The farm fields surrounding Oberly Road, southwest of Alpha, New Jersey, have been famous in eastern Pennsylvania and New Jersey for many years. They provide farm and grassland habitat not easily found in the eastern portion of our area anymore. Birders primarily go there for wintering raptors, owls, and passerines, but the area can be productive at any time of the year.

Birds. The species sought along Oberly Road can be found anywhere along its route. In the summer, Vesper, Grasshopper, Field, and Savannah Sparrows nest in the fields, as does an occasional Dickcissel. Eastern Meadowlarks are regular breeders here, too, as are many of the more common grassland species.

Oberly Road is known for a wintering population of Short-eared Owls, Northern Harriers, and Rough-legged Hawks. Even in years when these species are difficult to find elsewhere, they can often be found here. From late November through mid-April, a trip to the spot about an hour before dusk will usually turn up Harriers going down for the night and Short-eared Owls becoming active.

Because the fields are usually spread with manure during the cold months, northern passerines such as Horned Larks, Snow Buntings, and occasional Lapland Longspurs can be found in winter. Birders should watch for moving flocks as they work their way down the road. Once past the open fields and a farmhouse, there is a wooded area on both sides of the road that can be good for woodpeckers and sparrows.

Directions. Take I-78 east out of Pennsylvania to the first exit in Phillipsburg, N.J. (exit 3). Go left at the stop sign at the end of the ramp to the first stop light. Make a half-circle right-hand turn just past the sign labeled "22 West, 122 Alpha, U-turns." Cross over the road (Rt. 22) and go 1.0 mi. on New Brunswick Ave. to a stop light. Turn left onto Rt. 519 and follow 519 in and through Alpha for 1.7 mi. Immediately after passing under I-78, make a right turn onto Rt. 635 (Synder's Lane). Follow Rt. 635 1.3 mi. and turn right onto Oberly Rd.

Alternative directions: From the intersection of Rt. 22 with Rt. 33, take Rt. 22 east for 9.0 mi. (Where Rt. 57 splits off to the left, bear right to stay on Rt. 22). Turn right onto Rt. 519 and follow 519 for 2.7 mi., making sure to stay on 519 when it bears left at a flashing red light and then turns right sharply. Immediately after passing under I-78, make a right turn onto Rt. 635. Follow Rt. 635 1.3 mi. and turn right onto Oberly Rd.

Note. All birding must be done from the side of the road. The fields are privately owned, and the farmers do not like trespassers. They do not object to birders on the road.

38. Wy-Hit-Tuk Park

Description. This 22-acre Northampton County park, located along the Delaware Canal adjacent to the Delaware River just south of Easton, is named after the Lenni Lenape word for the river. A trail of approximately half a mile in length runs along the canal. Sycamores and other deciduous trees provide riparian habitat. Two foot bridges, one at the beginning and one at the south end of the park, allow one to cross the canal into the Delaware Canal State Park, which runs the entire length of the southeastern border of Pennsylvania between the canal and the river. The park itself is small, but its adjacency to this state park and other undeveloped areas on the east side of the river make it part of a large piece of continuous open space.

Birds. Warbling Vireos, and in some years, Yellow-throated Warblers, can be found in the sycamores. Orchard Orioles and a variety of other songbirds have been seen here, as well as Bald Eagles and Osprey over the river. The canal and river attract waterfowl, especially in winter and during migration.

Directions. From the intersection of I-78 with Cedar Crest Blvd. (Rt. 29), take I-78 east for 20 mi. to the last exit in Pennsylvania (exit 75, Easton-Philadelphia.) Turn right (south) off the ramp and take a quick left onto Cedarville Rd. Follow this road 1.5 mi. to the stop sign at Rt. 611. Turn right onto Rt. 611 South and follow it 1.3 mi to the park entrance on the left. The entrance is easily missed, so pay attention to mileage. (On 611, after passing under I-78, the park will be 0.4 mi. farther.)

Alternative directions: From Rt. 22, head east toward Easton and exit at 4th St. Follow the signs for Rt. 611 South. On 611 South, after going under I-78, go 0.4 mi. farther and turn left into the park entrance.

Notes. **(1)** Picnic areas and a restroom are located near the parking lot. **(2)** A trail guide is available at the information board near the lot. **(3)** For more information on Delaware Canal State Park, visit their web site at <www.dcnr.state.pa.us/stateparks/parks/d-canal.htm>.

39. Monocacy Nature Center

Description. The Monocacy Nature Center is a 20-acre sanctuary along the Monocacy Creek in Bethlehem. Trails lead to a pond about 3/4 of a mile from the parking lot. The trails pass through moist streamside woodland, beside a partially mowed field, and along wooded hillsides. The Sanctuary is owned and maintained by the City of Bethlehem with help from volunteers and organizations such as the Monocacy Creek Watershed Association and the Citizens Action Committee for the Monocacy Creek.

Birds. This small area attracts a surprising variety of warblers and other songbird migrants, as well as occasional ducks, shorebirds, and raptors. The sanctuary has a birdlist of 179 species including 34 warblers. Marsh Wren, Bobolink, Prothonotary Warblers, and Philadelphia Vireos have been seen here. The pond has held Black-crowned Night-Heron, Common Moorhen, and Common Snipe. Any part of the Nature Center can be rewarding during migration. Winter Wrens and Yellow-bellied Sapsuckers can often be found in winter.

Directions. From the intersection of Rt. 22 and Rt. 512, take Rt. 512 (Center St.) south for 1.6 mi. to Illick's Mill Rd. Turn right onto Illick's Mill Rd. Go 0.1 mi. to the parking lot on the left. The trail, marked by a hanging wooden sign, begins at the far end of the lot.

Notes. **(1)** Across the street from the parking lot is a more developed area with picnic tables. A restroom is located behind this area but is not open in all seasons. To walk there from the picnic area, head up the creek and cross the foot bridge just before the small dam and falls. To drive there from the main parking lot, turn right onto Illicks Mill Rd. and immediately turn left through a stone gate. Go 0.25 mi. down this drive to the red brick bath house on the left. A small parking area is just beyond it. Other restrooms are available at the municipal ice rink (in winter) just up Illicks Mill Rd. on the left or at the golf course in the same vicinity on the right. **(2)** It is best to avoid the trail along the stream during the opening week of trout season. **(3)** The railroad tracks are active; be alert for trains if birding near the tracks. **(4)** For more information, including sightings and seasonal highlights, visit the Monocacy Nature Center web site at <www.pipeline.com/~rlfreed/linda.htm>.

40. Nisky Hill Cemetery

Description. Nisky Hill Cemetery is a pleasant green space close to downtown Bethlehem. Its northern length and two sides are bounded by city streets and buildings, but at its south boundary a wooded hillside slopes down to the Lehigh River. Fruiting and flowering trees and shrubs, along with proximity to the hill and river, make this area attractive to birds despite its otherwise urban location. Paved, level paths provide easy walking.

Birds. The cemetery attracts songbirds and woodpeckers, especially during migration. Thrushes, including Swainson's and Hermit Thrush and Veery, can often be found in migration. Swallows and Chimney Swifts can be seen hunting over the river. Great Horned Owls have nested here. Cooper's Hawks have been seen, and, in recent years, occasional Wild Turkeys.

Directions. From the intersection of Rt. 22 with Rt. 512, take Rt. 512 (Center St.) south about 2.5 mi. to Elizabeth Ave. Turn left on Elizabeth Ave. and go 0.3 mi. to Linden St. Turn right onto Linden and follow it 0.8 mi. to Church St. Turn right onto Church; the cemetery will be on your left. Cars can be parked on the side streets or on Church St. west of the cemetery.

41. Sand Island

Description. Sand Island is a strip of land formed by the confluence of the Lehigh River, the Delaware and Lehigh Canal, and the Monocacy Creek. Most people enter Sand Island from the City of Bethlehem, but it can also be reached by cycling or hiking from the Lehigh Canal tow path.

The western portion of the land contains former industrial sites and is slated for re-development for recreational uses. Birders should head to the east (left) after crossing onto Sand Island. A trail of about 0.3 mi. runs along the Lehigh River, and several bridges along the way provide access to the tow path that runs on the other side of the canal.

Birds. Sand Island and the tow-path have a good variety and number of birds because of their proximity to three different kinds of riparian habitat: the fast-moving, wide Lehigh River, the narrow, rocky Monocacy, and the slow-moving, buggy canal. Walking either the Sand Island trails or the tow path puts you in the middle of these three habitats.

The area is good for water-loving birds: Osprey, Broad-winged Hawk, herons, swallows, diving and dabbling ducks in the river, and an occasional Bald Eagle. Indigo Buntings and Warbling Vireos are common along the canal, as are a variety of warblers during migration.

Directions. From the intersection of Rt. 22 with Rt. 378, take Rt. 378 south for 2.5 mi. to the Center City/Historic Bethlehem exit. Turn right off the exit onto Third Ave., then take the first right onto Union Blvd. At the first light, turn right onto Main St. Follow Main about 0.5 mi. through Bethlehem's shopping district and then downhill through an "S" curve just past the shops. At the intersection with Spring St., turn left to continue on Main St. One block later, at the four-way stop sign, go straight, over the bridge, onto Sand Island. Parking is available to the left after entering the island. If no spots are available, take the bridge back off the island and park in the large, city-owned lot just west of the bridge entrance.

Notes. (1) Sand Island is called Franklin Park on some maps. **(2)** Restrooms, open only in the summer, are located in the large brick building on the left after the first set of tennis courts. **(3)** Despite an alarming amount of litter, Painted and Snapping Turtles are abundant in the canal, as are fish.

42. Lehigh Mountain Uplands

Description. This 300+ acre nature preserve in Salisbury Township is tucked between Allentown, Fountain Hill, and the Lehigh River. The area is mostly forested hillside, but large utility tower paths create an extended swath of scrub and secondary growth. Part of the Uplands runs along the Lehigh River and provides good river views before the leaves emerge in spring.

A maze of trails extends from the ballfield near the parking lot into the woods. The trails that go to the east lead to an abandoned park and unused reservoir behind St. Luke's Hospital. To get to the utility lines, follow a trail that starts at the northwest corner of the ballfield and heads down the side of the mountain. The utility lines make a right angle bend. The section that runs north-south toward the Lehigh River is overgrown and difficult. The trail that heads toward the west under the power lines is easier, but still somewhat overgrown and usually very wet.

Birds. The Uplands are excellent in migration and also contain a good variety of breeding birds. Chestnut-sided and Blue-winged Warblers nest along the power lines, along with Indigo Bunting and Eastern Towhee. Worm-eating Warblers breed at the lower part of the mountain along Constitution Dr. and River Rd. The forest is home to breeding Broad-winged and Cooper's Hawks, as well as Wild Turkey, American Redstart, Ovenbird, Black-and-white Warbler, Scarlet Tanager, Rose-breasted Grosbeak, and most of the common woodland species. Summer records exist for White-eyed Vireo and Brown Creeper, and American Woodcock may still breed in abandoned, almost inaccessible fields just south of the power lines. Pileated Woodpecker is also a breeder here.

An island in the Lehigh River visible from the Uplands holds an active Great Blue Heron colony. The birds nest early in the spring, and the colony is best viewed in April when the activity level is high and before leaves on the trees obscure the view. The river can also be good for a variety of waterfowl during the winter.

Directions. To reach the main hiking trails, from Rt. 22, take Rt. 378 south 3.2 mi. to the bridge over the Lehigh River. Remain in the right lane as you cross the bridge. At the traffic light at the end of the bridge, there is a stone church on the left. From the stone church, continue 0.2 mi., staying in the right lane, to where Rt. 378 bears left and Broadway splits off from it. Bear right onto Broadway. Proceed 1.1 mi. and turn right onto Dodson St. Follow Dodson St. 0.4 mi. uphill to its end at a small parking area and ballfield.

To reach the area where the Great Blue Heron colony can be seen, from the intersection of Broadway with Dodson St., continue another 0.5 mi. on Broadway and turn right onto Weil St. Take Weil 0.5 mi. to a stop sign at Cardinal and continue to the left, which is Constitution Dr. At 0.1 mi. farther, there is a gate. If it is open, continue 0.8 mi. to railroad tracks. Cross the tracks, park, and look toward the river to the island.

If the gate is locked, you will need to approach from the other end of Constitution Dr. To do so, take Weil back to Broadway and continue on Broadway 2.1 mi. Turn right onto Constitution Dr. Follow Constitution, which becomes somewhat rough, 1.7 mi. to the railroad tracks.

To reach a good driving area for general river viewing, when following Rt. 378 south to the bridge over the Lehigh River, get in the left-hand lane as you cross the bridge. Exit at the 3rd St./ Rt. 412 exit toward the end of the bridge. At the end of the exit ramp is a Perkins restaurant. Turn left onto Riverside Dr. just past the entrance to Perkins. Follow the road across the tracks toward the water. The road runs about 1.5 mi. along the river.

Notes. (1) Bow hunting is allowed only at the Constitution Dr. end of the Uplands, and only during bow season. However, up to the 1990s, this area was open to all hunting. Some activity persists, so visitors should be cautious during hunting seasons. **(2)** The Uplands is an isolated area, and suspicious characters are occasionally encountered, especially along the river. It is best not to bird here alone.

43. South Mountain Park

Description. South Mountain Park is a small park owned by the City of Bethlehem, located on South Mountain above Lehigh University. It includes deciduous woods, stands of evergreens, a small creek, and open areas with and without bushes and shrubs. A number of informal trails crisscross the area.

Birds. The park attracts warblers in migration, including Ovenbirds. It has also been a good place, especially in the spring, for thrushes, Rose-breasted Grosbeaks, and Scarlet Tanagers among the evergreens. There may have been some decrease in birdlife here in recent years due to the park's popularity as a place to play disk (Frisbee) golf.

Directions. From the intersection of Rt. 22 with Rt. 378, take Rt. 378 south for 5.1 mi. to the crest of South Mountain. Turn onto South Mountain Dr.; to do so, you must first turn right and make a half-circle to the left, then proceed straight onto South Mountain Dr., as directed by signs. Go up South Mountain Dr. about 0.5 mi. and turn right into a drive at the crest of this hill (opposite the Channel 39 WLTV building on the left). Park and enter the park on the main path in the center near the Sanctuary sign. You will come to an open field with picnic tables. There are trails all around but mostly to the left.

Notes. (1) Disk (Frisbee) golf contests are scheduled year round, so this location is best for birding early or late in the day. **(2)** There are restrooms (though they may not be open in all seasons) and picnic areas with tables.

44. South Mountain Preserve (The Walter Tract)

Description. South Mountain Preserve is part of the 465-acre Robert Rodale Reserve that extends along the north side of South Mountain from I-78 to Emmaus. The preserve is a large, maturing second growth forest containing a spring and vernal ponds. The area is open to the public for hiking and birding. There is an extensive but unimproved trail system. Most of the trails are fairly level, but the few that climb South Mountain are very steep and rutted. The Robert Rodale Reserve has been identified by The Nature Conservancy as one of the most important natural areas in the Lehigh Valley. In addition to the portion of the reserve described here, almost any undeveloped area on the ridge can be rich in birds in migration and during the breeding season.

Birds. During spring migration, up to 27 species of warblers have been recorded in one day. In March and April, the east end of the upper field is a good spot for watching migrating hawks. Ten species of warblers, including Blue-winged, Worm-eating, Kentucky, and Hooded Warbler, and Louisiana Waterthrush, have bred here.

Directions. From the intersection of I-78 with Emaus Ave. in Salisbury Township, follow Emaus Ave. south for 1.2 mi. (Emaus Ave. becomes Dalton St. along the way.) Just past a 30 mph Y intersection, turn left onto Alpine St. Go three blocks to the end of the street. Park on Alpine St. or, if it is open, in the parking lot at Boro Line Park on the left.

Note. There are no restrooms.

45. Reservoir Park, Hellertown

Description. Hellertown's Reservoir Park is part of more than 500 acres of watershed owned by the Borough of Hellertown. (Local birders often refer to this park as the "Hellertown Reservoir," but the reservoir itself, about a mile away, does not have public access.) The park is a mostly wooded area with stands of tall oak, poplar, pines, hemlocks, and other coniferous and deciduous trees. There is a large fenced-in pond, several small ponds, and two streams on the property. To the left of the parking area, there is a large picnic pavilion with playing fields nearby. There are hiking paths around the pavilion and pond areas and in the woods beyond the ponds.

Birds. Year-round residents include common songbirds. Woodpeckers are well-represented. Pileated Woodpeckers are seen occasionally and are believed to nest in the area. In the winter months, Great Horned Owls can be heard in the late afternoon, and they nest in the area. Eastern Screech-Owls have also been heard. In recent years, Wild Turkeys have been seen. In the early spring, Eastern Phoebes nest in the pavilions and other small buildings. Spring migration attracts a good variety of warblers, Scarlet Tanagers, Wood Thrushes, and other migrant songbirds. Ovenbirds, American Redstarts, Black-and-white Warblers, Blue-winged Warblers, and Veerys nest in the area. Acadian Flycatchers and Kentucky Warblers are present in some years.

Directions. From the intersection of I-78 with Rt. 412 in Hellertown, take Rt. 412 south for 2.1 mi. through downtown Hellertown to Polk Valley Rd. (This road is immediately past a MacDonald's on the right and a small shopping plaza and bank on the left; it is also labeled "McAdoo Ave."). Turn left onto Polk Valley Rd. and go 0.7 mi. to the stop sign facing the Saucon Valley school complex. Turn right to continue on Polk Valley Rd. Continue on Polk Valley Rd. another 0.4 mi. Turn right onto Reservoir Rd. and go 0.3 mi. down a hill and across a small stone bridge. Bear left to the small parking area at the gated entrance to the park.

Notes. (1) An outhouse located near the pavilion is open May to October. **(2)** The main paths are paved or gravel and provide easy, though slightly hilly, walking. Wheelchair access is impeded by the entrance gate, when locked.

46. Lake Warren

Description. About 20 acres, little Lake Warren is part of undeveloped State Game Lands #56. The game lands, a mostly forested area, contain about 1,737 acres in Bucks County. Other habitats include edge, shrub, and marsh. The Delaware River is nearby. On both the southeast and southwest sides of the lake, there are unimproved roads and trails that run through the game lands.

Birds. The area is good for both woodland and wetland species. Bird reports include American and Least Bittern, Lesser Scaup, Ruffed Grouse, Virginia Rail, Sora, Semipalmated Plover, American Woodcock, Northern Saw-whet Owl, Brown Creeper, Willow Flycatcher, Prothonotary, Worm-eating, Hooded, and Kentucky Warbler.

Directions. From the intersection of I-78 with Rt. 412 in Hellertown, follow Rt. 412 south for about 12.2 mi. (passing through Hellertown, Leithsville, and Springtown). Turn left onto Church Hill Rd., just past Palisades High School on the left (You will pass Palisades Middle School 0.3 mi. on right before the turn). Go 1.5 mi. to the light at Rt. 611. Jog slightly to the left to cross Rt. 611 onto Center Hill Rd. Follow Center Hill Rd. 0.4 mi. and turn right onto Lake Warren Rd. Follow Lake Warren Rd. 1.2 mi. (crossing Kintner Hill Rd.), and turn left onto Nature's Way, a gravel road that is easy to miss. (Nature's Way is 0.1 mi. past the road marker for Rapp Creek.) The parking lot is 0.2 mi. at the end of the lane. The lake is to the left and there is a trail into the State Game Lands at the end of the parking area.

Notes. (1) Because the park is on state game lands, it is open to hunting in season. **(2)** On a recent visit in the second week of June, the lake was carpeted with water lilies blooming in shades of white, pink, and yellow. **(3)** For a full and varied birding day, consider a combined visit to the four birding spots in the area: Quakertown Swamp, Lake Towhee County Park, Nockamixon State Park, and Lake Warren.

47. Lake Towhee County Park

Description. Located in upper Bucks County, Lake Towhee County Park consists of 501 acres. The lake itself is 50 acres. During the summer, water lilies carpet a large portion of the water. Other habitats include creek area, forest, edge, and shrub.

Birds. Some of the species that have been reported include Great Egret, Green Heron, Mute and Tundra Swan, Blue-winged Teal, Gadwall, Wood Duck, Solitary Sandpiper, Barred Owl, Red-headed and Pileated Woodpecker, Yellow-bellied Sapsucker, Eastern Wood-Pewee, Eastern Phoebe, Veery, Blue-gray Gnatcatcher, Prairie Warbler, and Louisiana Waterthrush. Red-shouldered Hawks have nested here, and Brant are occasionally seen. Migratory birds use this as a resting area.

Directions. From the intersection of I-78 and Rt. 309, take Rt. 309 south for about 9 mi. to the intersection with Rts. 313 and 663 in Quakertown. Turn left onto Rt. 313 and follow it east for about 4.8 mi. Turn left onto Rt. 563 and take it north for about 2.2 mi. Turn left onto Old Bethlehem Rd. Continue 2.3 mi. to the park entrance on right. Access to the water is from the parking lot at the end of the long entrance drive.

To get to the Lake Towhee Nature Center, turn right out of the park entrance onto Old Bethlehem Rd and proceed 0.7 mi. Turn right onto E. Saw Mill Rd. The nature center is 0.8 mi. on the right.

Notes. (1) There are restroom facilities. **(2)** The park is open year-round from 8:00 a.m. to sunset. **(3)** Canoes and kayaks are allowed with proper permits.

48. Nockamixon State Park

Description. Nockamixon State Park in upper Bucks County covers 5,283 acres including the 1,450 acre Lake Nockamixon, a freshwater impoundment. In addition to the 7-mile long lake, habitats include abandoned farmfields, meadows in different stages of succession, mature hardwood forests, coniferous plantations including larch and White Pine, and marshy areas.

Located just southeast of Quakertown and bordered by Rts. 313, 563, and 611, plus Ridge Rd., most areas of the park are easily explored. With a 2.8 mile paved bike trail, 27 miles of coved and largely wooded shoreline, a 20-mile network of equestrian trails, and 3.5 miles of foot trails, this quiet and relatively undeveloped state park provides excellent birding.

Birds. Nockamixon is large enough to attract any northeastern possibility, from an irruptive Snowy Owl to a Bald Eagle. The diversity of habitats has attracted close to 200 bird species, with five accidentals. Twenty-seven warbler species and seven thrushes have been recorded. Birds of prey pass through during their migrations, and Osprey can sometimes be seen fishing. Cliff Swallows nest under the bridges. The marina near the docks is good for gulls, and Snow Buntings are sometimes seen along the beach near that area in fall and winter.

Check stands of pines for Red-breasted Nuthatch and Long-eared Owl (along roads to Fishing Pier and Kellers Church). Brushy fields have yielded Yellow-breasted Chat, Orchard Oriole, and Indigo Bunting. Waterfowl that have been attracted to the lake include Tundra and

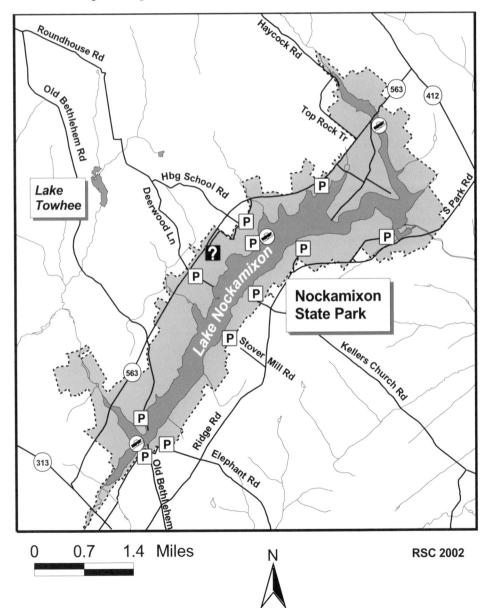

0   0.7   1.4 Miles   N   RSC 2002

Mute Swans, Blue-winged and Green-winged Teal, Snow Goose, Ruddy Duck, and Red-breasted Merganser. Spotted and Solitary Sandpipers and American Woodcock (in moist woodlands) are among the shorebirds that have visited.

Directions. From the intersection of I-78 with Rt. 309, take Rt. 309 south for about 9 mi. to the intersection with Rts. 313 and 663 in Quakertown. Turn left onto Rt. 313 and follow it east for about 4.8 mi. (You will pass through downtown Quakertown and then return to more rural areas.). Turn left onto Rt. 563 and follow it north 3.4 mi. to the park office and main entrance on the right. Good access points to the water are the fishing pier (just before the main entrance), the marina and Haycock and Tohickon boat launch areas (past the main entrance along 563), and the Three Mile Run boat launch area (on the opposite side of the lake). All are well-marked.

Alternative directions from the Bethlehem area: From the intersection of I-78 with Rt. 412 in Hellertown, follow Rt. 412 south for about 13.5 mi. (passing through Hellertown, Leithsville, and Springtown) to Rt. 563. Turn right onto Rt. 563 and follow it south 4.2 mi., passing the Haycock and Tohickon boat ramp and the marina entrances, to the main entrance and park office on the left.

Notes. (1) A recreational guide (which includes a map) is available at the park office. **(2)** The park is open daily from 8:00 a.m. to sunset. The day use area is open between April 1 and October 31. From November through March, the day use area is closed to cars but open for walking. For more information, call (215) 529-7300 or visit the park web site at <www.dcnr.state.pa.us/stateparks/parks/nock.htm>. **(3)** The park can be very crowded in summer. **(4)** There are 10 restrooms scattered throughout the park. The restrooms in the day use area and the marina are closed during the winter. The Haycock and Tohickon boat launch and the fishing pier restrooms are open year-round. **(5)** A kayak or canoe is an ideal way to explore all the marshy fingers and coves of Lake Nockamixon. Either bring your own or rent one at the boat rental concession. Call (215) 538-1340 for information. Launching facilities are open all year. **(6)** Approximately 3,000 acres of Nockamixon State Park are open to hunting. Use caution when entering these areas during open seasons. **(7)** State Game Land #157, also a hunting area, abuts the northeast border of the state park. Haycock Mountain, the second highest point in Bucks County, is within the Game Land and accessible via a hiking trail.

49. Quakertown Swamp

Description. Located just south of its namesake town in upper Bucks County, the Quakertown Swamp is a unique inland wetland area. The 400-acre swamp remains relatively undisturbed. The heart of the swamp is bisected by a railroad embankment, which provides an elevated view. Habitats in addition to the wetland include deciduous forest, edge, shrub, and a small pond.

Birds. A Pennsylvania Breeding Bird Census identified 74 nesting species in the swamp, of which 14 are considered rare breeders. The swamp contains the largest Great Blue Heron rookery in eastern Pennsylvania. Other breeding species include Marsh Wren, Virginia Rail,

American Bittern, Yellow-billed and Black-billed Cuckoo, and Yellow and Blue-winged Warblers.

Other species of note include Least Bittern, Osprey, Red-shouldered Hawk, Sora, Common Moorhen, Common Snipe, Common Nighthawk, and Swamp Sparrow. Visit the pond area for Wood Duck, Eastern Phoebe, Ruby-crowned Kinglet, and Blue-gray Gnatcatcher. During migration, look for Palm Warblers and other passerines.

A path leads to the pond from the parking area described below. To reach the swamp, walk east (to the left) along Rich Hill Rd. about 0.4 mi. until you reach the railroad overpass. (Be careful of traffic.) Climb up the bank, watching out for poison ivy, and turn left. Walk alongside the railroad tracks in toward the swamp for about half a mile.

The Great Blue Heron rookery can be seen from Muskrat Rd. just past the parking area (look to the left). Viewing is best in the spring before the vegetation leafs out. The area along this road is also good for rails.

Directions. From the intersection of I-78 with Rt. 309, take Rt. 309 south for about 9 mi. to the intersection with Rts. 313 and 663 in Quakertown. Continue on Rt. 309 another 2.0 mi. and turn left at the light onto Tollgate Rd. In 0.3 mi., turn right at the T intersection onto Old Bethlehem Pike. In 0.9 mi., turn left onto Rich Hill Rd. Follow Rich Hill Rd. 1.2 mi. and turn left onto Muskrat Rd., then turn right into the State Game Lands parking area almost immediately.

Notes. (1) The portion of the swamp described here is part of State Game Lands #139 (the rest is on private land). The game lands consist of 265 acres. It is easily accessible to the public and is open year-round. Hunting is allowed. **(2)** Prime visiting times are April through June, particularly in the early evening. **(3)** One of the two railroad tracks is still active. Be alert for trains when walking alongside the tracks, and avoid standing or walking on the tracks themselves. **(4)** In recent years the vegetation height along the tracks has increased, making viewing conditions less favorable than in the past. **(5)** The site has been designated as an Important Bird Area (IBA) by Pennsylvania Audubon Society.

50. Unami Creek Valley

Description. The Unami Creek Valley in western Montgomery County offers excellent woodland birding between April and October. Most of the area is floodplain forest, but it also contains dryer mixed and oak forest, small meadows, and Red-cedar stands. Several man-made dams along the length of the creek provide habitat for herons, ducks, and other water birds.

Birds. The following provides a tour beginning at Unami Creek Park. To reach the starting point of the tour, see **Directions**.

From the parking lot of Unami Creek Park, in spring and early summer, scan the large shade trees along the creek for Eastern Kingbird, Cedar Waxwing, and Baltimore and Orchard

Orioles. The shrubs on the opposite side of Swamp Creek Rd. may hold Winter, Carolina, and House Wrens in the appropriate seasons, and a variety of sparrows. Walk Swamp Creek Rd. upstream for 0.4 miles to a stone-arch bridge on the right. There is no shoulder, so watch carefully for traffic. This stretch of road contains the famous Sumneytown vulture roost. At times the roost has held over 200 birds (including 50+ Black Vultures), although the birds have become somewhat unpredictable in recent winters. A conspicuous band of white-wash (and tell-tale odor) is a good sign that the birds have been present. In the spring, this stretch of road can yield an impressive array of migrant songbirds and other species. Look and listen for Broad-winged Hawk, Pileated Woodpecker, Eastern Wood-Pewee, Acadian Flycatcher, Yellow-throated Vireo, and nearly any eastern warbler. Most notable of the warblers are Northern Parula, Louisiana Waterthrush, and Yellow-throated Warbler. While still considered rare, this last species has become almost annual at this spot.

At the bridge, scan overhead for raptors, swallows, and other species. Northern Rough-winged Swallows nest under the bridge and can be seen at close range as they perch on the wires. From this spot, either continue walking north along Swamp Creek Rd. or return to your vehicle.

After crossing the stone-arch bridge, enter the parking lot on the immediate left. (During the last two weeks of April, this lot can be filled by trout fishermen.) Scan the trees at the edge of the lot for Blue-gray Gnatcatchers, vireos, and warblers. Check the creek here for Wood Ducks (spring and summer) and Hooded Mergansers (winter).

The next stretch of Swamp Creek Rd. is 1.1 mi. in length. There are small pull-offs roughly every 0.2 mi., but be aware of high road shoulders and oncoming traffic, and exercise caution entering and exiting. Proceed along Swamp Creek Rd. through an area of mature floodplain and mixed dryer forest. This area hosts six woodpecker species (all but Red-headed), and is the last stronghold of the Pileated Woodpecker in western Montgomery County. Watch overhead for vultures, Sharp-shinned, Cooper's, Red-shouldered, and Broad-winged Hawks. Eastern Screech- and Great Horned Owls are fairly common here, and Barred Owl is extremely rare. Both cuckoo species can be found here in spring and summer, as can a variety of songbirds including vireos, thrushes, Scarlet Tanagers, Rose-breasted Grosbeaks, and warblers. Just beyond a concrete dam/spillway, park in the small lot on the left. When not filled with scouts in rowboats, this impoundment may yield herons, Wood Ducks, and Belted Kingfishers. Snags along the shoreline can harbor flycatchers, and the dense understory and shrub layer is good for thrushes and warblers.

From this parking lot, travel 0.4 mi. to a powerline crossing. A walk up the steep slope here may produce Yellow, Blue-winged, Chestnut-sided, and Prairie Warblers, Yellow-breasted Chat, Indigo Bunting, Eastern Towhee, and various sparrows. (If you would rather not make the climb, turn right on Payne Rd. and drive to the same high-tension lines.) From the powerline crossing, continue north on Swamp Creek Rd. for 0.5 mi. and turn right on Knuckles Rd. There is a small pull-off on the immediate right. Walk upstream on Swamp Creek Rd. for 0.2 mi. to a stone-arch bridge on the left (Price Rd.). From the bridge, scan the large sycamore trees and wires for various raptors and songbirds. Returning to the car, listen for Acadian

Flycatcher, Kentucky Warbler, and Worm-eating Warbler which are all fairly reliable here. Wild Turkey are possible in any season along the Unami Creek corridor. They can act almost tame at times, as they are descended from pen-reared birds. Their wildness returns each spring, however, when they have broods of young in tow.

To continue the tour, take Knuckle Rd. 0.1 mi. to the first intersection (Scott Rd.) and turn left. Follow Scott for 0.9 mi. (called Hill Rd. at the end) to the stop sign at White's Mill Rd. Turn right and proceed for 0.6 mi. to the mill pond on the left. The pond often holds Wood Ducks, Ring-necked Ducks, and other waterfowl. Red-shouldered Hawk and Pileated Woodpecker are both possible here, as is nearly any woodland songbird in spring. (Note: this parcel was recently acquired as "open space" by the township. Its future as a birding site is uncertain.) To complete the tour, return to Swamp Creek Rd. and turn left. Follow it back to Geryville Pike and PA Route 63.

Directions. The Unami Creek Park parking lot is the starting point of the tour. From the intersection of I-78 with Rt. 29 (Cedar Crest Blvd.), take Rt. 29 for 14.7 mi. to the intersection with Rt. 663. (Note that Rt. 29 makes a sharp right in Emmaus and a sharp left at the traffic light at the village of Hereford where it splits from Rt. 100; follow the signs.) From the intersection with Rt. 663, continue another 4.7 mi. on Rt. 29 to Rt. 63 in Green Lane. Bear left onto Rt. 63 and follow it east for 1.3 mi. Turn left at the Sumneytown Hotel onto the Geryville Pike. Go 0.2 mi. and turn right on Swamp Creek Rd. Park in the lot on the immediate right at Unami Creek Park.

Notes. (1) Most of the land along Swamp Creek Road is private property (including the scout camp). Birders should not trespass and should bird from the road shoulders. Be alert for oncoming traffic. **(2)** The site has been designated as an Important Bird Area (IBA) by Pennsylvania Audubon Society.

APPENDIX A

Pennsylvania Ornithological Records Committee
Review List June 2001

The Review List contains species that are considered rare or accidental in Pennsylvania. The committee requests written details, including descriptions, photos or video/sound recordings if possible, of all records of the following species for review for possible inclusion on the official state list documenting the ornithological history of Pennsylvania. (Please note county exemptions).

Pacific Loon, Northern Fulmar, Black-capped Petrel, Cory's Shearwater, Leach's Storm-Petrel, Northern Gannet, Brown Pelican, Great Cormorant (exempt in Bucks, Delaware, Philadelphia), Anhinga, Magnificent Frigatebird, Tricolored Heron, Cattle Egret, White Ibis, Glossy Ibis, Roseate Spoonbill, Wood Stork, Black-bellied Whistling-Duck, Pink-footed Goose, Greater White-fronted Goose (exempt in Berks, Bucks, Chester, Delaware, Lancaster, Lebanon, Montgomery, Philadelphia), Ross's Goose (exempt in Berks, Bucks, Chester, Delaware, Lancaster, Lebanon, Montgomery, Philadelphia), Cinnamon Teal, Eurasian Wigeon (male only exempt), Tufted Duck, King Eider, Harlequin Duck, Barrow's Goldeneye, Masked Duck, American Swallow-tailed Kite, Mississippi Kite, Swainson's Hawk, Gyrfalcon, Yellow Rail, Black Rail, Clapper Rail, King Rail, Spotted Rail, Purple Gallinule, Snowy Plover, Wilson's Plover, Piping Plover, American Oystercatcher, Black-necked Stilt, Whimbrel (Erie exempt), Black-tailed Godwit, Hudsonian Godwit, Marbled Godwit, Surfbird, Red Knot, Purple Sandpiper (Erie exempt), Buff-breasted Sandpiper, Ruff, Red-necked Phalarope, Red Phalarope, Pomarine Jaeger, Parasitic Jaeger, Laughing Gull (exempt in Erie and the lower Delaware and Susquehanna rivers), Franklin's Gull (Erie exempt), Little Gull (Erie exempt), Black-headed Gull, Mew Gull, Thayer's Gull, Black-legged Kittiwake, Ross's Gull, Sabine's Gull, Gull-billed Tern, Royal Tern, Roseate Tern, Arctic Tern, Least Tern, Sooty Tern, Black Skimmer, Dovekie, Thick-billed Murre, Ancient Murrelet, Band-tailed Pigeon, Eurasian Collared-Dove, White-winged Dove, Common Ground-Dove, Northern Hawk Owl, Great Gray Owl, Boreal Owl, Chuck-will's-widow, Rufous Hummingbird, Black-backed Woodpecker, Pacific-slope Flycatcher, Say's Phoebe, Vermilion Flycatcher, Western Kingbird, Scissor-tailed Flycatcher, Loggerhead Shrike, Violet-green Swallow, Boreal Chickadee, Bewick's Wren, Sedge Wren, Northern Wheatear, Mountain Bluebird, Townsend's Solitaire, Bicknell's Thrush, Varied Thrush, Bohemian Waxwing, Black-throated Gray Warbler, Townsend's Warbler, Kirtland's Warbler, Swainson's Warbler, Summer Tanager (exempt in Greene), Western Tanager, Green-tailed Towhee, Spotted Towhee, Lark Sparrow, Lark Bunting, LeConte's Sparrow, Saltmarsh Sharp-tailed Sparrow, Nelson's Sharp-tailed Sparrow, Seaside Sparrow, Harris' Sparrow, Golden-crowned Sparrow, Black-headed Grosbeak, Blue Grosbeak (exempt in Bucks, Chester, Delaware, Lancaster, Philadelphia and York), Lazuli Bunting, Painted Bunting, Western Meadowlark, Yellow-headed Blackbird, Brewer's Blackbird, Bullock's Oriole, Brambling, Pine Grosbeak, and Hoary Redpoll.

APPENDIX B

New Jersey Bird Records Committee Review List

The New Jersey Bird Records Committee exists to collect and maintain data pertaining to records of scarce or rare birds reported in the state of New Jersey. The committee requests written details, including descriptions, photos or video/sound recordings if possible, of all records of the following species for review for possible inclusion on the official state list.

Pacific Loon, Eared Grebe, Western Grebe, Black-browed Albatross, Black-capped Petrel, Buller's Shearwater, Audubon's Shearwater, White-faced Storm-Petrel, White-tailed Tropicbird, Red-billed Tropicbird, Brown Booby, American White Pelican, Anhinga, Magnificent Frigatebird, White Ibis, White-faced Ibis, Roseate Spoonbill, Wood Stork, Fulvous Whistling-Duck, Greater White-fronted Goose, Ross' Goose, "Black" Brant, "Richardson's" Canada Goose, "Eurasian" Green-winged Teal, Cinnamon Teal, Tufted Duck, Barrow's Goldeneye, Swallow-tailed Kite, Swainson's Hawk, Eurasian Kestrel, Gyrfalcon, Yellow Rail, Purple Gallinule, Sandhill Crane, Northern Lapwing, Mongolian Plover, Wilson's Plover, Black-necked Stilt, Spotted Redshank, Eskimo Curlew, "Eurasian" Whimbrel, Long-billed Curlew, Black-tailed Godwit, Bar-tailed Godwit, Little Stint, Curlew Sandpiper, Eurasian Woodcock, Long-tailed Jaeger, Great Skua, South Polar Skua, Franklin's Gull, Thayer's Gull, Ross' Gull, Sabine's Gull, Ivory Gull, Arctic Tern, Bridled Tern, Sooty Tern, Large-billed Tern, White-winged Tern, Whiskered Tern, Common Murre, Thick-billed Murre, Black Guillemot, Atlantic Puffin, Band-tailed Pigeon, Common Ground-Dove, White-winged Dove, Northern Hawk Owl, Boreal Owl, Black-backed Woodpecker, Say's Phoebe, Ash-throated Flycatcher, Gray Kingbird, Scissor-tailed Flycatcher, Fork-tailed Flycatcher, Violet-green Swallow, Cave Swallow, Boreal Chickadee, Rock Wren, Bewick's Wren, Northern Wheatear, Mountain Bluebird, Townsend's Solitaire, Varied Thrush, Sage Thrasher, Sprague's Pipit, Bohemian Waxwing, Loggerhead Shrike, Bell's Vireo, Virginia's Warbler, "Audubon's" Yellow-rumped Warbler, Black-throated Gray Warbler, Townsend's Warbler, Swainson's Warbler, Western Tanager, Black-headed Grosbeak, Painted Bunting, Green-tailed Towhee, Spotted Towhee, Bachman's Sparrow, Cassin's Sparrow, Black-throated Sparrow, Lark Bunting, Henslow's Sparrow, Le Conte's Sparrow, Golden-crowned Sparrow, "Gambel's" White-crowned Sparrow, Harris' Sparrow, Dark-eyed Junco, Smith's Longspur, Chestnut-collared Longspur, Western Meadowlark, Brewer's Blackbird, Bullock's Oriole, Brambling, and Hoary Redpoll.

APPENDIX C

Rare Bird Report Details

- ❏ SPECIES (common and scientific name)
- ❏ Subspecies (if known)
- ❏ NUMBER OF INDIVIDUALS _____ SEX (ES) _____
- ❏ AGE(S) AND PLUMAGE(S) (e.g. immature; adult in breeding plumage; year for gulls; basic or alternate if you prefer those terms; state of molt if applicable)
- ❏ DATE OF OBSERVATION _____ TIME _____
- ❏ LOCATION (city, borough, township)
- ❏ EXACT SITE (e.g. name of park, lake, road)
- ❏ OBSERVER REPORTING: Name, address, e-mail (optional), and phone (optional)
- ❏ OTHER OBSERVERS (only those who saw and identified the bird with you)
- ❏ HABITAT (e.g. mowed field, woodland edge, any other details)
- ❏ DISTANCE TO BIRD
- ❏ VIEWING CONDITIONS (sky, weather, position of sun relative to you)
- ❏ OPTICAL EQUIPMENT USED
- ❏ DESCRIPTION (Include as much detail as you observed – size relative to other species present; "jizz"= e.g. posture, body shape, and proportions; colors and patterns of plumage; bill, eye, and leg characteristics; other features relevant to this individual)
- ❏ BEHAVIOR (be as detailed as possible about what the bird was doing)
- ❏ VOCALIZATIONS
- ❏ SUPPORTING EVIDENCE IF ANY:
- ❏ Photograph _____ Video recording _____ Audio recording ____ Drawing _____
- ❏ Photographer/recorder/illustrator (include address)
- ❏ Please include a copy of the photograph or recording with your report, and accompany it with a complete written documentation even if the identification is obvious to you. If you made a drawing, please include it.
- ❏ SEPARATION FROM SIMILAR SPECIES (how you eliminated others)
- ❏ DISCUSSION – Anything else relevant to the observation that will aid the committee in evaluating it.
- ❏ PREVIOUS EXPERIENCE WITH THIS AND/OR SIMILAR SPECIES
- ❏ ARE YOU POSITIVE OF YOUR IDENTIFICATION? (why or why not)
- ❏ REFERENCES CONSULTED: During observation and after observation
- ❏ DATE OF THIS REPORT

Send reports to:

For Pennsylvania
Reports should be sent to the current secretary for the Pennsylvania Ornithological Records Committee, Pennsylvania Birds magazine, or the Pennsylvania Society for Ornithology. The current contact information can be found at <www.pabirds.org> or through your local bird club or area bird watchers.

For New Jersey
Reports should be sent to the New Jersey Birds Records Committee. The current contact information can be found at <www.princeton.edu/~llarson/njrc.html>, or contact the New Jersey Audubon Society Headquarters, 9 Hardscrabble Road, PO Box 126, Bernardsville, New Jersey 07924, (908) 204-8998 <www.njaudubon.org>.

APPENDIX D

American Birding Association's Principles of Birding Ethics

Everyone who enjoys birds and birding must always respect wildlife, its environment, and the rights of others. In any conflict of interest between birds and birders, the welfare of the birds and their environment comes first.

CODE OF BIRDING ETHICS

1. Promote the welfare of birds and their environment.

1(a) Support the protection of important bird habitat.

1(b) To avoid stressing birds or exposing them to danger, exercise restraint and caution during observation, photography, sound recording, or filming.

Limit the use of recordings and other methods of attracting birds, and never use such methods in heavily birded areas, or for attracting any species that is Threatened, Endangered, or of Special Concern, or is rare in your local area;

Keep well back from nests and nesting colonies, roosts, display areas, and important feeding sites. In such sensitive areas, if there is a need for extended observation, photography, filming, or recording, try to use a blind or hide, and take advantage of natural cover.

Use artificial light sparingly for filming or photography, especially for close-ups.

1(c) Before advertising the presence of a rare bird, evaluate the potential for disturbance to the bird, its surroundings, and other people in the area, and proceed only if access can be controlled, disturbance minimized, and permission has been obtained from private land-owners. The sites of rare nesting birds should be divulged only to the proper conservation authorities.

1(d) Stay on roads, trails, and paths where they exist; otherwise keep habitat disturbance to a minimum.

2. Respect the law, and the rights of others.

2(a) Do not enter private property without the owner's explicit permission.

2(b) Follow all laws, rules, and regulations governing use of roads and public areas, both at home and abroad.

2(c) Practice common courtesy in contacts with other people. Your exemplary behavior will generate goodwill with birders and non-birders alike.

3. Ensure that feeders, nest structures, and other artificial bird environments are safe.

3(a) Keep dispensers, water, and food clean, and free of decay or disease. It is important to feed birds continually during harsh weather.

3(b) Maintain and clean nest structures regularly.

3(c) If you are attracting birds to an area, ensure the birds are not exposed to predation from cats and other domestic animals, or dangers posed by artificial hazards.

4. Group birding, whether organized or impromptu, requires special care.

Each individual in the group, in addition to the obligations spelled out in Items #1 and #2, has responsibilities as a Group Member.

4(a) Respect the interests, rights, and skills of fellow birders, as well as people participating in other legitimate outdoor activities. Freely share your knowledge and experience, except where code 1(c) applies. Be especially helpful to beginning birders.

4(b) If you witness unethical birding behavior, assess the situation, and intervene if you think it prudent. When interceding, inform the person(s) of the inappropriate action, and attempt, within reason, to have it stopped. If the behavior continues, document it, and notify appropriate individuals or organizations.

Group Leader Responsibilities [amateur and professional trips and tours].

4(c) Be an exemplary ethical role model for the group. Teach through word and example.

4(d) Keep groups to a size that limits impact on the environment, and does not interfere with others using the same area.

4(e) Ensure everyone in the group knows of and practices this code.

4(f) Learn and inform the group of any special circumstances applicable to the areas being visited (e.g. no tape recorders allowed).

4(g) Acknowledge that professional tour companies bear a special responsibility to place the welfare of birds and the benefits of public knowledge ahead of the company's commercial interests. Ideally, leaders should keep track of tour sightings, document unusual occurrences, and submit records to appropriate organizations.

APPENDIX E

Birding Records: How to Keep Them Using a Field Notebook

Recording field observations and your ideas is essential to increasing knowledge about birds and the natural world in general. The status and abundance of a species can change over time due to natural conditions, as well as the result of the actions of humans. Accurately recording these changes over time is essential if future authors are to be able to revise and improve upon our knowledge of birds in the Lehigh Valley, our state, nation, and the world. Additionally, only by accurately documenting these changes can birds be used to serve as useful indicators to conserve these animals that we gain pleasure from seeing and studying, and perhaps to reveal the need to modify a practice that adversely affects the environment overall. Birds are proven indicators of environmental health worldwide, but their value for this purpose can only be realized if appropriate records are kept of their numbers at specific locations. The more detailed the notes, the more useful they will be to others. What follows is just one recommended means of documenting your field experiences or your thoughts about them. In other words, it is a tool used to document your ideas and interpretations of what you observe, measure, think, and generally learn about the perceived world around you. It requires the creation of a notebook, a field notebook, and every entry must be written for someone else to read, that is, written in a way that is clear, concise, and correct. There are many notebook styles, but one standard format that has gained wide acceptance is the field notebook system of Joseph Grinnell (1877-1939), as modified by his students. Dr. Grinnell was Professor and Director of the Museum of Vertebrate Zoology at the University of California at Berkley where he served from 1908 to 1938. You are invited to practice his system and his challenge to better serve the birds you enjoy and your fellow birders who will have the opportunity to learn and be rewarded by your efforts. His challenge, as applicable and in need of continued repetition today as any other, is: *"No notebook this day, no sleep this night."*

Hardware. The field notebook is a standard three ring binder 20.3 x 25.4 cm (8 x 10 in) that will accept 15.2 x 24.1 cm (6.0 x 9.5 in) loose-leaf paper. Obtain the highest quality rag paper available, typically 25% rag content. Commercial paper of this size is printed without margins. Using a straight edge, draw a 3.8 cm (1.5 in) margin on the left side of each facing page; entries are primarily made on only one side, the facing page. Historically, serious field note takers through more than half of the twentieth century used a metal quill pen dipped frequently into a bottle of Higgins Eternal Ink. From the 1930s to the present, technical pens that held waterproof India ink were used for their convenience in holding a large amount of ink. A technical drawing pen with a point size between 0.30 to 0.40 mm is recommended, but point sizes as thick as 0.70 mm are acceptable. Such pens require regular attention and cleaning if they are to provide good service. Alternatively, making entries much easier, there are now ballpoint pens with waterproof black ink available (0.6 mm Pentel K105, Hybrid). The ink must be intensely black and waterproof. If in doubt about a pen and ink, once dry, ink should be tested to determine its ability to withstand submerging in water, alcohol, formaldehyde, and ammonia. In addition to the binder and pen with waterproof ink, obtain a pencil (3H or 4H is recommended), and a small pocket note pad approximately 9.5 x 15.6 cm (3.8 x 6.1 in) to carry into the field. On cold days the ink in ball-point pens will freeze and you will need a pencil to take notes. For many activities field notes are initially taken in the note pad or on specially designed data sheets and later transcribed into the field notebook. Note pad notes must be transcribed into your field notebook as soon as possible; again, frequently repeating Grinnell's advice to yourself and others is always an appropriate reminder: *"No notebook this day, no sleep this night."*

Organization and Format. In its most complete form, the field notebook is organized into three sections, separated by prominent dividers: Journal, Species Accounts, and Catalog. Not all sections are needed, but all field notebooks minimally have a Journal section where all types of entries can be recorded. The Species Accounts and Catalog sections are optional, and used to better organize and facilitate the recording and retrieval of the information they contain.

Prior to writing notes in any section, each page must have margins drawn and other areas specifically formatted. For all sections and all pages your full name, preferably, or your initials and the year must be written at an angle, or parallel to the line, in the upper left corner and between the top edge and the first line. Field Notebooks are kept for one year, and a new one is started on 1 January of the new year. In the top middle of the page, between the top edge and the first line, write the word Journal on every page of the Journal section. In this same position, the Common Name and, directly below it, the properly formatted Scientific Name is written on every page of the Species Accounts section. In this same position, Catalog is written on every page of the Catalog section. Only the Journal section has typical Arabic page numbers; they are written in the upper right corner. In the Species Accounts section, all entries for a specific species are kept in chronological order, and entries of different species are kept in taxonomic order throughout the section. Species Accounts entries are the same as narrative Journal entries (described below). A Species Accounts section aids a note taker or more serious bird student by placing documented accounts of a select number of species in one location to facilitate their use. The Catalog section is used to record repetitive data strings, such as specimen, bird banding, or location records that are more easily read when placed in a tabular format. Catalog records are entered in chronological order by subject.

All entries begin with the date (written as 18 February or February 18) placed to the left of the left margin, and the day written directly below the date. On the same line as the date but to the right of the margin, a title that meaningfully describes the entry is written and a wavy line drawn under it. Directly below the title write the location where the activity took place and enclose it in parentheses; this information is required for a field entry but it is optional for some narrative entries, such as entries that record your thoughts about an idea or one in which you might speculate on any number of events you witness in the field. If an entry carries over to additional pages, write the date, day, and a short title with wavy underline on each subsequent page. Additionally, place the word Continued under the day to the left of the margin and after the short title but do not extend the wavy line under the word Continued placed after the short title. Where the title of a narrative entry is a descriptive label, the title of a field entry has a specific format that includes: a site name, county, and state where the records were taken. The location in parentheses directly below the field entry title must direct the reader from a known and prominent landmark, such as a road junction or post office.

There are two types of Journal entries: narrative and field. The narrative entry is the most common, and as the name implies, they are descriptions of conversations, interviews, procedures, ideas, readings or the results of other library work, or other types of events or information the writer seeks to record for reference and to share with the reader. Before completing an entry, a valuable practice is to test yourself by rereading your account and evaluating its effectiveness: will a reader be able to repeat your activities, obtain an accurate description of your observations, and clearly understand your intentions? To further aid the reader, avoid using any abbreviations and always remember that you are writing for someone else to read. Where a narrative entry can be uniquely creative in recording your activities, a field entry is highly structured and more applicable for birding notes taken in the field. A field entry includes introductory information describing the location, time afield, travel (by vehicle and foot if applicable), habitat (ideally, a detailed description to include percentage of habitat coverage), detailed weather conditions (minimally: temperature, wind speed and direction, precipitation, percentage of cloud cover), and initial comments labeled Remarks (general weather assessment or purpose for visiting the site). This introductory description is presented as a paragraph, and it is followed by a blank line and the title Species List in the center of the page. Another blank line and then the listing, in taxonomic order, of the species and their numbers that you recorded while birding. The list is written in two or three columns. After the list, another blank line and then a summary line is written. The summary line contains the number of species recorded, the total number of individuals recorded, and time spent recording. Place a circle around the summary line, followed by another blank line, followed by the title Comments just to the right of the left margin. After the Comments title write the details of your activities, detailed notes on any unidentified birds, your impressions and interpretations, and any other appropriate information you wish to share with a reader.

Front and Back Matter. Although optional, to further organize and aid yourself and your readers, additions called front and back matter are prepared at the end of a calendar year. The front matter consists of a Table of Contents and Abbreviation pages. The back matter is an Index. These pages are formatted, like other pages for other sections, with your name, year, and margins drawn on every page. Front matter numbering is different, and consists of small Roman numerals placed at the bottom center of each page. The title Table of Contents is written where Journal, the species name in the Species Accounts, or Catalog is written in their respective sections. Below the Table of Contents title, is a single-line listing of each entry of the field notebook by section, and includes entry date (to left of margin), entry title (right of margin) followed by the beginning and ending pages of the entry. Following the Table of Contents is the Abbreviation page or pages with the title placed in the same position as and continuing the same numbering system from the Table of Contents. Under the title Abbreviations, include a short paragraph informing the reader that the abbreviations you used in your field notebook follow in alphabetical order, and if at any time they come upon an abbreviation in the field notebook that they do not recognize, they should return to these pages to obtain its definition. Although especially challenging, if your energy and organizational skills permit, you will greatly aid yourself and your reader by preparing an Index to appear as back matter after your last field notebook entry. Place the word Index in the top center of the page, and inside the right margin, in alphabetical order, list all key words and species and the section and pages upon which they occur in your notebook.

Protect Your Records. Keep your notebook safe, and make arrangements to have them deposited in a museum or library when your note taking days are over. For added protection consider binding your field notebooks. The 3.8 cm (1.5 in) margin on the left side of each facing page is required to facilitate eventual binding.

References. The following books and articles provide additional detailed information on why and how to keep natural history records.

Hall, E. R. and K. R. Kelson. 1959. The mammals of North America. Vol. II. Ronald Press. New York, 1037-1038 pp.

Herman, Steven G. 1986. The naturalist's field journal: a manual of instruction based on a system established by Joseph Grinnell. Buteo Books, Shipman, VA, 200 pp.

Remsen, J. V., Jr. 1977. On taking field notes. American Birds 31(5): 946-953.

Short, L. L., Jr. 1970. Bird listing and the field observer. California Birds 1: 143-145.

(This Appendix is modified and taken from Biology of Birds and Ornithology course materials of D. Klem, Jr., Department of Biology, Muhlenberg College, Allentown, Pennsylvania.)

APPENDIX F

Organizations and References

Organizations

Lehigh Valley Audubon Society
P.O. Box 290, Emmaus, Pa 18049
Web Site: www.lehigh.edu/~bcm0/lvas.html
Local Hotline: 610-252-3455

New Jersey Audubon Society Headquarters
9 Hardscrabble Road, Bernardsville, N. J. 07924
Web Site: www.njaudubon.org
Telephone: 908-204-8998

Pennsylvania Society for Ornithology (Pennsylvania Birds magazine)
2469 Hammertown Road, Narvon, Pa 17555-9726
Web Site: www.pabirds.org

PABirds (A bird discussion web site for Pennsylvania)
E-mail Address: PABIRDS@LIST.AUDUBON.ORG
(Send an e-mail requesting information on how to join)

American Birding Association
P. O. Box 6599, Colorado Springs, CO 80934-6599
Telephone: 719-578-0607
Web Site: www.americanbirding.org

Cornell Laboratory of Ornithology
P.O. Box 11
Ithaca, New York 14851
Telephone: 1-800-843-BIRD
Web Site: www.birds.cornell.edu

Reference Books

Atlas of Breeding Birds in Pennsylvania. 1992.
Daniel W. Brauning, Editor
ISBN: 0-8229-3692-5

The Birds of Pennsylvania. 2000.
Gerald M. McWilliams and Daniel W. Brauning
ISBN: 0-8014-3643-5

LITERATURE CITED

American Ornithologists' Union. 1998. Check-List of North American Birds, 7th Edition American Ornithologists' Union, Washington, D. C.

American Ornithologists' Union. 2000. Forty-second Supplement to the American Ornithologists' Union Check-List of North American Birds. Auk 117: 847-858

Boyle, William J., Jr., Robert O. Paxton, and David A. Cutler. 1992. Hudson-Delaware Region. American Birds 46(3): 397-402.

McWilliams, G.M., and D. W. Brauning. 2000. The Birds of Pennsylvania. Cornell University Press, Ithaca, New York.

Morris, B. L., R. E. Wiltraut, and F. H. Brock. 1984. Birds of the Lehigh Valley Area. Lehigh Valley Audubon Society, Emmaus, Pennsylvania.

Nagy, A. 1971. 1970 Curator's Report. Hawk Mountain Sanctuary Association News Letter to Members 43: 3-10.

Paxton, Robert O., P. A. Buckley, and David A. Cutler. 1977. Hudson-Delaware Region. American Birds 31(5): 979-984.

Poole, E. L. 1964. Pennsylvania Birds, An Annotated List. Livingston, Narbeth, Pa.

Scott, F. R. and David A. Cutler. 1972. Middle Atlantic Coastal Region. American Birds 26(4): 745-748.

Thomas, Lester S. 1953. Birds of Bucks County, Pennsylvania. Cassinia 40: 2-26.

144

INDEX

NOTES